RELEASE
YOUR DESTINY,
RELEASE
YOUR ANOINTING

EXPANDED
EDITION

D0972866

AVAILABLE FROM DESTINY IMAGE PUBLISHERS

RELEASE
YOUR DESTINY,
RELEASE
YOUR ANOINTING

EXPANDED
EDITION

T.D. JAKES

DESTINY IMAGE® PUBLISHERS, INC.

P.O. Box 310, Shippensburg, PA 17257-0310

"Speaking to the Purposes of God for this Generation and for the Generations to Come."

This book and all other Destiny Image, Revival Press, MercyPlace, Fresh Bread, Destiny Image Fiction, and Treasure House books are available at Christian bookstores and distributors worldwide.

For a U.S. bookstore nearest you, call 1-800-722-6774.

For more information on foreign distributors, call 717-532-3040.

Reach us on the Internet: www.destinyimage.com.

Trade Paper ISBN 13: 978-0-7684-3220-6

Hardcover ISBN 13: 978-0-7684-3397-5

Large Print ISBN 13: 978-0-7684-3398-2

Ebook ISBN 13: 978-0-7684-9074-9

For Worldwide Distribution, Printed in the U.S.A.

1 2 3 4 5 6 7 8 9 10 11 / 15 14 13 12 11 10

CONTENTS

FOREWORD

Ever since his early days as a small-town preacher, T.D. Jakes has understood the power of the anointing. He learned the secrets of embracing the love and power of God for his life and ministry. As his current ministry attests, he still embraces the anointing to deliver the most life-changing messages spoken anywhere in the world today.

If you are like most believers, you want to learn these secrets so that you, too, may pour God's anointing into a thirsty and dying world. Like Bishop Jakes, you have learned that the world's only hope is the refreshing and healing power of God's Presence that flows from those who yield themselves to this anointing.

God has a calling and a place for every person, including you! T.D. Jakes discovered his calling—and anointing—early in his life, and it has led him to free the captives, heal the wounded, and be a voice in the wilderness for millions of desperate and hungry Christians worldwide.

Here, for the first time in a single volume, you can learn from T.D. Jakes the secrets to releasing the anointing within you. It's not hard. It only requires understanding why the anointing works. With choice wisdom from the best-selling *Woman, Thou Art Loosed!*,

Can You Stand to be Blessed (also available under the title *Insights to Help You Survive the Peaks and Valleys*), *Naked and Not Ashamed* (also available as *It's Time to Reveal What God Longs to Heal*), and *Anointing, Fall on Me*, you can become all that God has planned for you, no matter what your present circumstances say you can or cannot do.

Take a bold step into the anointing-filled future awaiting you.

—Don Nori Sr., Publisher
Destiny Image Publishers

INTRODUCTION

I feel compelled to present scriptural truth on the power of the anointing of the Holy Ghost that is simple, timely, and applicable to your life. I believe this is a very timely book—one that will equip you to meet the devil's end-time onslaught to thwart the plan of God.

I believe that we're in the beginning stages of the greatest revival this world has ever known. In order for us to carry out the plan of God, we must realize that divine intervention and not human effort will usher in this end-time revival. Christians must know that their lives with God can be full of new experiences every day. Instead of merely enduring our salvation, we can enjoy the fullness that God has provided in the Holy Ghost—by releasing our anointing.

If you have been saved by the grace of God, you have a calling on your life. God may want you to be a pastor, an evangelist, or a missionary. He may call you to be a light in the business world. You may have been apprehended by the hand of God to write books, lead people in worship, or raise godly children.

You need to realize that these gifts and callings were not placed in your life to lie dormant. Only by the power of the Holy

Ghost will you see them fulfilled. This book will show you how to meet challenges, realize your full potential, and release your anointing.

If you apply these practical truths in your life, you will begin to experience a new freshness in God. The plans that you have hoped to fulfill all your life will become reality. Do you long for certain things in God? Does your sanctified soul stir at the thought of doing exploits for God? A sense of destiny causes you to determine, "No matter what I must go through, I can and will make it!"

These truths on the Holy Ghost will take you to higher heights and deeper depths in God. Get ready to experience a new joy and power that will change your life—and the lives of others.

Chapter I

POWER FOR LIVING

Why is it so important to pray with the power of the Holy Ghost? All too often, our spirit is willing, but our flesh is weak. We need God's help to overcome the tug of our carnal nature.

Being filled with the Holy Ghost places the power of God at our disposal to carry out the work of the Kingdom. Soon after being baptized in the Holy Ghost, most believers notice a marked change in their ability to pray and walk in God's anointing.

Humankind Is Body, Soul, and Spirit

Apostle Paul wrote: *"And I pray God your whole spirit and soul and body be preserved blameless unto the coming of our Lord Jesus Christ"* (I Thess. 5:23). This Scripture shows us the three parts of humankind: body, soul, and spirit.

If these three parts were the same, Paul never would have prayed that they each would be wholly preserved. If we want to have a successful prayer life and reach our full potential with God, then each of these parts must be understood and put in their place.

Each of these parts affects our prayer life. If we were only spirit, the blessings of prayer would be unrestrained, without hindrance. But we also have to deal with our body and soul.

The words *wholly* and *preserved* are significant. *Wholly* means to completely, absolutely reach the limit or potential. *Preserved* means to guard, to watch, to keep an eye on, to keep something in its place. As we pray, we must contend with these three parts. Each element plays a significant role in the success or failure of our prayer life:

1. *Body.* The body entails our flesh and its appetites. The flesh never wants to pray. The flesh never awakens you with a desire to seek God. The flesh is at enmity with God and does not understand His ways. This is why no one can please God in the flesh. Because the flesh will never come up to the expectations of the Spirit, we must discipline the flesh to be subject to what we know is right. The flesh will sit back and say, "You don't have to pray. If it's going to happen, then it will happen." But we must go into combat to get certain things. We must bombard the gates of Heaven to obtain certain things, and the body never wants to do this.

2. *Soul.* The soul of man is sandwiched between our body, which never wants to pray or do right, and our spirit, which desires God and spiritual things. The soul entails our emotions, feelings, weaknesses, and our past. An ongoing, progressive, renewing work occurs in your soul. When we pray with our soul, we pray with our intellect and an understanding to the

best of our ability. But to go into deep spiritual warfare, we must go beyond our logic and our intellect.

3. *Spirit.* When you were lost, your spirit was *"dead in trespasses and sins"* (Eph. 2:1). Now that you are saved, however, your spirit has been quickened, which means to vitalize, to cause to live, to be vibrant and strong. As the Holy Ghost begins to have an intimate relationship with our spirit, we begin to produce the *"fruit of the Spirit"* (Gal. 5:22,23). The Holy Ghost wants to know you in an intimate way; He doesn't want just a surface relationship.

Intimacy results in fruit, or offspring: *"Adam knew his wife again; and she bare a son, and called his name Seth"* (Gen. 4:25).

Apostle Paul wrote, *"that I may know him"* (Phil. 3:10), which implies a close relationship—one that causes us to partake in His experiences. But you can't know Christ in resurrection power until you know Him in His sufferings and death. Our old man must be crucified with Him daily, as we are being changed from glory to glory.

Apostle Paul knew Jesus in the pardon and forgiveness of sin, but still longed to know Him intimately. For this to occur, two things had to happen:

1. *"Forgetting those things which are behind"* (Phil. 3:13). These were not all bad or questionable activities, but they were not satisfying, either. They left Paul crying out for more of God.

2. *"Reaching forth unto those things which are before"* (Phil. 3:13). Paul wanted to press toward the mark for the

prize of the high calling of God in Christ Jesus. He wanted to become spiritually intimate with Jesus to produce fruit.

Why Speak in Tongues?

This is a good question, asked by many intelligent people. Why should anyone speak in tongues? Tongues merely express the language of God. In order for us to reach the will of God for our lives, we must be able to communicate with God.

Speaking in tongues is not a strange new doctrine. In fact, it's been around for hundreds, even thousands, of years. God poured it out at the inception of the Church.

Before we cover several scriptural reasons for this practice, I would like to share an example that highlights the importance of speaking in tongues.

A CB radio gives you the ability to speak to other people, providing you are on the same frequency. Different people use different channels for a variety of reasons. Whatever channel you use to transmit or receive a message, the transmitter and the one receiving must be on the same channel and have the squelch turned up loud enough to hear. CB radios also have a special channel for emergencies. Any time you need the police or emergency assistance, you can switch to this frequency and no one else can monitor your conversation.

This may seem like a crude analogy, but in the spirit world many messages are being transmitted. The Bible says that satan is the *"prince of the power of the air"* (Eph. 2:2). If we stay on the same frequency, he can pick up our transmissions. But satan cannot monitor the emergency channel. His squelch cannot tune in, because it is just a bunch of static to him. He cannot make out what we are saying. Praying in the Spirit is a frequency that satan cannot pick up.

Bypassing Satan's Radar

And I heard a loud voice saying in Heaven, Now is come salvation, and strength, and the Kingdom of our God, and the power of his Christ: for the accuser of our brethren is cast down, which accused them before our God day and night (Revelation 12:10).

Since satan is the prince of the power of the air and comes before the presence of God, he constantly surveys our prayer life. No wonder we experience such adversity and opposition when we try to get close to God. To make our way to the throne of God, we must push past the enemy's surveillance.

For we wrestle not against flesh and blood, but against principalities, against powers, against the rulers of the darkness of this world, against spiritual wickedness in high places (Ephesians 6:12).

Let me use another illustration. In the first Iraq War, the United States and its allies knew that they were up against some of the most modern, up-to-date defenses in all the world.

The war was waged in two parts. During the first part, known as Desert Watch or Desert Shield, the United States flew reconnaissance flights to monitor the movement and the strengths and weaknesses of the enemy.

Because of these reconnaissance flights, we learned that Iraq had employed the most modern, state-of-the-art radar systems. The United States knew if we were to be successful—with limited casualties—we would have to somehow bypass Iraq's radar system. This was achieved by using stealth bombers, which enabled us to mount an attack without being detected on radar.

On the first night of the attack, the major bombardment was almost over before Iraq even realized what had happened.

When you pray in the Spirit, you go before the throne of God undetected by satan because you speak mysteries to Him. Your prayers are like stealth bombers that bypass satan's detection.

Praying in the Spirit enables you to pray healing, delivering, yoke-breaking, devil-stomping prayers without being shot at. You can go into God's presence and receive ammunition to shake the gates of hell. That's why satan fights people from praying in the Spirit. He confuses people regarding this truth because he knows he doesn't have a weapon to defend against it.

Switching Channels

The apostle Paul uses the word *tongues* (plural) to show his multiplicity of languages. *"Though I speak with the tongues of men and of angels..."* (I Cor. 13:1).

Sometimes we need to speak in our natural language according to our heritage. Sometimes, however, our natural language is no match for the warring spirits between earth and the throne of God.

When prayers in our natural language are being intercepted and shot down, Paul tells us to switch channels. Allow the Holy Ghost within you to speak out on earth what Heaven is speaking into your spirit. This is praying in tongues, or praying in the Spirit.

Satan understands the language of men. When we pray about a certain thing, our adversary causes principalities and powers in the atmosphere between earth and the throne of God to intercept our words. He attacks the very thing we pray about.

Satan does not understand the language of Heaven. God's ways, which are so much higher than our ways, include praying in tongues. This leaves satan confused as to how to attack us. He may assign an evil spirit to attack our prayer life and report back to him so he can make a counterattack. But when we pray in the Spirit, or pray in tongues, we frustrate his plans.

Remember that tongues are spiritual and not fleshly. Satan works through our flesh. When our prayers switch from an earthly, fleshly, carnal language to a secondary, spiritual, heavenly language, satan is confused.

The believer is built up as the Holy Ghost pleads the life, the power, the joy, and the victory of God into your spirit. Hallelujah for the ability to speak out from earth what the Holy Ghost is speaking in from Heaven!

Interceding With Groans

Speaking in tongues places a great arsenal of spiritual weaponry at your disposal. Not knowing this, however, many believers struggle in prayer and intercession.

> *Likewise the Spirit also helpeth our infirmities: for we know not what we should pray for as we ought: but the Spirit itself maketh intercession for us with groanings which cannot be uttered. And he that searcheth the hearts knoweth what is the mind of the Spirit, because he maketh intercession for the saints according to the will of God* (Romans 8:26-27).

Romans 8:26 contains a word that is often overlooked, and that is the very first word, likewise. The word means "in like manner," or "to be similar to."

> *For we know that the whole creation groaneth and travaileth in pain together until now. And not only they, but ourselves also, which have the firstfruits of the Spirit, even we ourselves groan within ourselves, waiting for the adoption, to wit, the redemption of our body* (Romans 8:22-23).

It points back to the two previous times the word groan is used in that chapter. Romans 8:22 refers to the groan of creation waiting for the redemption and restoration of this earth. Romans 8:23 refers to the groans of Christians as we await the completion of our redemption, the receiving of our new body.

Apostle Paul uses the same word for the groans of the Holy Ghost (see Rom. 8:26). The word *groanings* means "to groan with a sigh, or a sense of lamenting."

This was very familiar to the Old Testament prophets. When they got in tune with the nature and character of God, they often expressed themselves in unusual ways. Their intercession for the people could be described as wailing, howling, or lamenting. They were speaking a language outwardly that God was speaking inwardly to them.

We cannot understand the language of God in our own intellect.

I like to explain it like this: When a child who cannot talk plainly wants something, he or she may be able to speak only portions of words. A stranger may not understand, but the child's mother can make out the language. Even though the baby talk is barely intelligible, she understands the need. Taking a bunch of stammering, broken remarks, she interprets the language to meet the need.

Sometimes in order to get what you need from God, you must go from one language (our human intellect) to another language (the Holy Ghost).

Help in Prayer

The Holy Ghost stands alongside us to assist, to cause one to stand, to cause one to achieve. It means "one who stands in covenant with." In essence, the Holy Ghost stands by your side to not only plead the covenant of God, but also to cause you to attain what the covenant provides for you.

He does this in four ways:

1. He assists us through our infirmities.

2. He assists in that He knows.

3. He assists us with intercessions.

4. He assists us with Heaven's language.

Help Through Infirmities

The Spirit "helpeth our infirmities," which means He stands alongside as an ally, one waiting in the wings who is willing and able to assist us. We need help because *the spirit indeed is willing, but the flesh is weak*" (Matt. 26:41).

The word *infirmities* means "inability to produce results." Opposition prevents you from receiving what God has provided for you in His covenant. The Holy Ghost helps us and gives us a breakthrough.

Help in Knowing How to Pray

He assists us in that He knows. The Spirit is very knowledge-able about things that perplex us. *"For we know not what we should pray for"* (Rom. 8:26). We don't always know what is right. As we allow the Holy Ghost to saturate and to permeate our lives, He begins to tell us how to pray for certain things.

For instance, whom should you date? Whom should you marry? Where should you go to church? In what ministry should you serve? Sometimes you'll want to speak or do something, and the Holy Ghost will caution you, "Don't say or do that." He assists you when you don't have clear direction.

Help With Intercessions

He assists us with intercessions. As Jesus our Mediator pleads us to God, the Holy Ghost who knows the very mind of God pleads God to us. "He maketh intercession for us." *Intercession* means that the Holy Ghost will meet with us. He comes into our situation and speaks into our spirit as one who interviews another.

We don't have the ability to produce results and to get our breakthrough. Even if we did have the ability, we are still void of knowledge because we *"know not what we should pray for."* The Holy Ghost will get us to admit our frailties. Then He will fellowship with us and assist us in what to do. As the Holy Ghost intercedes, He merely speaks into earth what He has already heard spoken in the counsels of Heaven.

This is why Jesus often repeated a truth He wanted to reveal: *verily, verily,* or *truly, truly*—once in the heavenlies by divine sanction, and once in the earth to carry out the divine sanction.

Help With Heaven's Language

He assists us with Heaven's language. The Spirit pleads the will of God to us. *"Because he maketh intercession for the saints according to the will of God"* (Rom. 8:27). As creation groans, it speaks a language that only God can interpret. The saints of God sometimes groan with broken, stammering remarks.

Sometimes all we can do is lay before God, not knowing what to do or say. We need to be full of the Holy Ghost and listening to Him, because He will plead God's will to us. We just have to be able to hear. *"He that hath an ear, let him hear what the Spirit saith unto the churches"* (Rev. 2:7).

The Holy Ghost Relays What Heaven Sends

John 16:13 presents some of the greatest truths ever revealed to the Church. Jesus said the Holy Ghost would do four things:

1. He will guide you into all truth.

2. He will speak truth to you, but He will not speak of Himself.

3. He will show you all truth concerning things to come.

4. He will speak into you what He hears Heaven speaking into Him.

We must be able to hear what the Holy Ghost is saying to be able to release our anointing. But it is equally important to know that the Holy Ghost hears what to speak to us. He never breaks the chain of command from Heaven. How can we know that what the Holy Ghost says is reliable?

First, the Holy Ghost is one with God. He will never speak anything that is not sanctioned by the Word. Second, God, who cannot lie, searched Heaven and earth for someone to confirm His covenant and swear to its authenticity. When He could find no one else to meet the criteria of His holy demands, God swore by Himself. Now the Holy Ghost freely speaks a sworn oath and covenant into the hearts of Spirit-filled believers who can hear His voice.

Jesus said, "whatsoever he heareth, he speaketh." That means the Holy Ghost speaks into you what Heaven has already decreed.

Build Up Yourself

In the following passage we find some of the simplest and most profound truths in all the Word of God. But everything hinges on the truth stated in verse 20:

But ye, beloved, building up yourselves on your most holy faith, praying in the Holy Ghost, keep yourselves in the love of God, looking for the mercy of our Lord Jesus Christ unto eternal life. And of some have compassion, making a difference: And others save with fear, pulling them out of the fire; hating even the garment spotted by the flesh (Jude 20-23).

We can build up ourselves, cultivate a sense of expectancy about the coming of the Lord, have compassion on those who have fallen, and be moved with zeal to make a difference in the lives of those who have spotted their garments.

Let's look at the ability to "build up." The word *build* is an architectural word that means "to cause a building to stand." It means "to lay a good foundation." In the natural realm, it is always important to leave yourself the ability to add on to your building in case you need to expand in the future. If you have outgrown your spiritual house, the Holy Ghost gives you the resources to add on to meet your demands.

If you have more ministry, then you have a place to house it, to build on. Are there weak areas in the structure? Build them up. You do this by praying in the Holy Spirit. This will build up your faith so that you can stand against Goliath and know that your God is bigger than the giant who defies you.

When God got ready to bless Elijah, His ultimate will was for the prophet to stand on Mt. Carmel, which means "fruitful ground." But the blessing came progressively as he went to the brook Cherith, where he drank from its waters and was fed by ravens. One day, however, the brook dried up and no longer met his needs. The word *Cherith* means "to make covenant with." God made a covenant, proving not only Himself to Elijah, but Elijah to Himself.

Next, God sent Elijah to a widow in *Zarephath*, which means "to refine as in a melting pot." Gold is not pure in its original form. It must be refined, which is done by heating it to boiling. The heat separates the raw substance from its impurities, which surface and are skimmed off. God does the same for us, using the heat of trials to separate the gold from the dross in our lives.

God leads you through a progressive path, but the ultimate goal is to be on Mt. Carmel and be fruitful. He wants you to be able to call fire down from Heaven, to see into the Spirit as Elijah saw, and to persevere in prayer until God intervenes in your situation. The answer to your drought may appear to be a cloud the size of a man's hand, but you know a refreshing rain is about to fall.

This is why Christians from all denominations are being filled with the Holy Ghost. Having outgrown the tradition of their past experiences, they have passed the tests at Cherith and Zarephath and are ready to go to Mt. Carmel.

If you feel a hunger to go on with God, the Holy Ghost is telling you that your current spiritual house is too small. He is urging you to build on your present foundation. In order to do this, however, we must pray in the Holy Ghost.

More Benefits

Unlike giving a message in tongues in a public meeting, which edifies other people, praying in tongues edifies you. We often walk into a nice church building, recognizing it as being a tremendous edifice. It simply is a great place for dwelling, meeting, communing, and fellowship.

Praying in tongues does at least five things for you individually:

1. Praying in tongues gives you the ability to talk to God alone, frustrating the devil.

2. Praying in tongues edifies the person praying (see I Cor. 14:4).

3. Praying in tongues helps you put on the armor of God.

4. Praying in tongues builds up a wall of defense.

5. Praying in tongues helps you relieve anxiety.

Frustrating the Devil

"*He that speaketh in an unknown tongue speaketh not unto men, but unto God*" (1 Cor. 14:2). This gives you the ability to bypass all others and go into the presence of God. The Old Testament equivalent would be to go into the holy of holies and commune directly with God.

Your adversary brings certain things against you to discourage and cause you to lose focus. Praying in tongues enables us to bypass his radar system.

Edification for the Person Praying

The word *edify* means "to build up, to build on, to establish a structure." As you pray in tongues, you enlarge your borders. If you have more ministry than prayer life, then add on. If you have outgrown where you are, then add on.

Your complexes will vanish as the Holy Ghost imparts confidence. Your fears will vanish as the Holy Ghost builds you up. Your past failures and sins will be dealt a decisive blow by the Holy Ghost. This change will take every weak area in your structure and begin to brace and strengthen it, giving you glorious victory.

You may not even notice the change taking place, and you might not even realize it's the Holy Ghost doing the work quietly and internally. But it won't be long before what is happening on the inside begins to manifest itself on the outside. As you learn to pray in the Holy Ghost, it will just happen automatically.

As you come into a deeper relationship with God, you will find that you cannot survive on a "Now I lay me down to sleep" prayer. Your prayer life will have to match your ministry and commitment to Spirit-filled living.

But ye, beloved, building up yourselves on your most holy faith, praying in the Holy Ghost (Jude 20).

Praying in the Holy Ghost shores up the foundation of our faith.

The best defense against disease is our natural immune system, which has been designed by God to help us ward off the enemies of our body and diseases that come against us. But the immune system must be kept strong and vibrant by eating right, getting plenty of rest, and exercising. Many of us are at our own lowest ebb spiritually and have become susceptible to anything that comes our way. But if we pray in the Holy Ghost, we will be built up, enabling us to fight off sin and discouragement.

Putting on the Armor of God

And take the helmet of salvation, and the sword of the Spirit, which is the word of God: Praying always with all prayer and supplication in the Spirit, and watching thereunto with all perseverance and supplication for all saints (Ephesians 6:17-18).

Praying in tongues will help you put on the armor of God. Many Christians feel this spiritual preparation is like choosing their clothes for the day from their closet. The apostle Paul mentioned our warfare, our enemies, and our armor, which covers every vital part of a soldier: the helmet (our mind); the breastplate (our heart); the girdle of truth (the truth of God's Word, upon which the whole armor rests); the shield of faith, which kept the soldier walking forward and never turning his back, which was exposed; the preparation of the gospel on our feet (our walk).

This armor dresses us for any occasion. But after describing the armor piece by piece, Paul goes right from verse 17 to verse 18 without stopping. It's as if he's saying, "This is how you get the armor: praying always in the Spirit." Praying in the Holy Ghost clothes us from head to foot with the armor of God. Yes, praying in the Spirit arms you with an arsenal that will cause you to stand. Hallelujah for the ability to pray in the Holy Ghost!

Building up a Wall of Defense

When the enemy shall come in like a flood, the Spirit of the Lord shall lift up a standard against him (Isaiah 59:19).

Yes, there are times when the enemy invades our lives. He will come into your mind; he will come into your marriage; he will come into your ministry. He comes in like a flood and desires to devour you and anything that has been born of God in your life.

The Holy Spirit stands by as your ally. When the enemy comes in like a flood, the Spirit shall lift up a standard against him. He provides you with a place of defense, a place of shelter, a place of refuge, a place to hide.

Job's life is a good example of this. When God praised Job's integrity, satan pointed out: *"Hast not thou made an hedge about him, and about his house, and about all that he hath on every side?"* (Job 1:10).

The adversary asked permission to touch all that Job had. Satan came in like a flood, destroying his sons, daughters, servants, and livestock. Not satisfied with this, satan asked permission to afflict Job's body. God set a limit, however, and said, *"Save his life"* (Job 2:6).

Praying in the Spirit sets up a wall of defense that satan cannot penetrate. The Spirit will lift up the wall of the blood of Jesus and say, "satan, you can't touch this!"

Relief from Anxiety

Praying in tongues helps you relieve anxiety. Jesus told his disciples, *"Come ye yourselves apart into a desert place, and rest a while"* (Mark 6:31).

Praying in the Spirit allows you to *come apart* before you come apart. Many of you are under severe pressure. You are tense, battle weary. Like the disciples, you need a solitary place to rest awhile.

Praying in the Spirit pulls us into an experience with God and enables us to release our anointing. It's not surprising that Paul wondered whether he was in the body or out of the body. The apostle saw and heard things unlawful for a man to speak. God in the Spirit takes us to paradise, pulling us apart from the pressures of the world before we are pulled apart.

A piece of material does not come apart suddenly. It unravels bit by bit. If you don't repair it, a small tear can cause the whole garment to come apart. Praying in the Spirit brings us to that solitary place with God to help cope with stress, pressure, and anxiety. If your life is falling apart, your need is similar to the woman with the issue of blood. She wanted to touch the hem of Christ's garment. She realized the hem was where all loose ends were put back together. This is what praying in the Spirit will do.

The apostle Paul wrote, *"What is it then? I will pray with the spirit, and I will pray with the understanding also: I will sing with the spirit, and I will sing with the understanding also"* (I Cor. 14:15). "I will pray with the spirit," means that you rely on the Holy Ghost to guide you as you pray. He will speak, but we must listen. When we pray with the Spirit, we are praying with the knowledge of God's will:

Likewise the Spirit also helpeth our infirmities: for we know not what we should pray for as we ought: but the Spirit itself maketh intercession for us with groanings which cannot be uttered (Romans 8:26).

We also pray with the insight of the Spirit:

And he that searcheth the hearts knoweth what is the mind of the Spirit, because he maketh intercession for the saints according to the will of God (Romans 8:27).

When we pray in the Spirit, we pray with fervency and intensity as the Spirit gives us the unction to focus on what we are praying for and to diligently seek God.

But without faith it is impossible to please him: for he that cometh to God must believe that he is, and that he is a rewarder of them that diligently seek him (Hebrews 11:6).

When we say, "I will pray with the understanding," we are saying that as we pray by the unction and leadership of the Holy Ghost, we pray a prayer that will have meaning as the same Holy Ghost interprets to us the things that we have spoken.

Sometimes we have no knowledge of how to pray because the things that we confront are bigger than we are. They are deeper than our human logic can comprehend. That's why we need to pray within the spirit realm, which is bigger than any problem, weakness, or dilemma we face. We also need to ask God to interpret to us the things that we have spoken through the auspice of the Holy Ghost. As He reveals them to us, we will gain an understanding.

We Need the Anointing

Sometimes we don't know what to say. Our hearts are crushed; our spirits are overwhelmed. We know that we need a touch. We know the area that needs to be touched, but we don't always know what to say.

Have you ever been so overwhelmed, so overcome, that all you can do is groan? Maybe you can only say, "Jesus, help me," or "I need You, Lord." That's when we need to change our language, and let the Helper work, as we discussed earlier in this chapter. We need to wait on the Holy Ghost because He knows how to pray—and what to pray. The Holy Ghost will always pray in alignment with the will of God (see Rom. 8:27).

The anointing of the Holy Ghost doesn't always bring chills or goosebumps. It isn't always charged with emotion. The anointing, however, brings power.

The Old Testament high priest knew there was only one place where he could see and experience a manifestation of God's glory, and that was in the holy of holies. That's where God promised to show Himself and commune with His people (see Exod. 25:17-22).

In these last days, satan and all his cohorts are waging a final onslaught against the Church. We must know God in a way in which we have never known Him before. Within some of you are miracles, unborn babies, ministries, and gifts. We all have callings.

Because of circumstances—perhaps something beyond your control; perhaps because of your faults, failures, or your past life—satan has told you that your baby, your gift, your ministry, must be aborted. But satan is a liar. Scripture tells us, "*The gifts and callings of God are without repentance*" (Rom. 11:29). You need to get to where you can see the raw, undiluted presence of God and His anointing. Only then can you release your anointing to bring glory to His Kingdom.

You Can Make It!

What encourages me when I go through the storms of life? I look in the Word of God and find that someone else has already been there and made it through. We are surrounded by witnesses:

> *Wherefore seeing we also are compassed about with so great a cloud of witnesses, let us lay aside every weight, and the sin which doth so easily beset us, and let us run with patience the race that is set before us* (Hebrews 12:1).

In each instance, however, these saints had to get to a certain place before they saw the manifestation of God.

Noah endured a torrential downpour that flooded the earth for months, but he had a place that gave him access to God. On the third level of the ark a window gave him access to the heavenlies. In the midst of his storm, he found solace and peace:

> *A window shalt thou make to the ark, and in a cubit shalt thou finish it above; and the door of the ark shalt thou set in the side thereof; with lower, second, and third stones shalt thou make it* (Genesis 6:16).

Jacob struggled for years with who he was, compared to who he wanted to be. His wrestling climaxed when he got to Jabbok, which means "to pour out, to empty." Jacob went alone to Jabbok, the place of struggle where he wrestled with an angel. Divinity met with humanity, and Jacob's thigh was put out of joint. When he arrived at Jabbok, the patriarch was Jacob (swindler, supplanter, cheater), but after the struggle, his name was Israel (prince of

God). It was a place of power, as God gave him power with Himself and man (Gen. 32:21-29).

Moses struggled with his leadership responsibilities over the nation of Israel. The demands of the multitude taxed Moses to the point of exhaustion. Moses asked God for a manifestation of His glory. But before Moses could see this manifestation, he had to get to a certain place. Hidden in the cleft of a rock, Moses saw the afterglow of God's glory—but only after he got to that place.

How the Anointing Works

If you're a believer in Christ, you have some type of calling on your life. You may be a pastor or a leader in the church. You may have a specific gift that needs to be stirred up.

Like Jacob, you may be struggling with who you are. Some of you may be wrestling with your past. You need to know that there is a place with God of yoke-breaking anointing. Let's look at two passages of Scripture for some timely truths:

Behold, how good and how pleasant it is for brethren to dwell together in unity! It is like the precious ointment upon the head, that ran down upon the beard, even Aaron's beard: that went down to the skirts of his garments; as the dew of Hermon, and as the dew that descended upon the mountains of Zion: for there the Lord commanded the blessing, even life for evermore (Psalm 133:1-3).

And it shall come to pass in that day, that his burden shall be taken away from off thy shoulder, and his yoke from off thy neck, and the yoke shall be destroyed because of the anointing (Isaiah 10:27).

- *The anointing flows from the head down* (see Ps. 133:2). Jesus is the head. His anointing is flowing, but we must be in alignment (in fellowship) with Him.

- *The anointing will be "as the dew of Hermon"* (see Ps. 133:3a). The Israelites knew the dew of Mt. Hermon and Mt. Zion was heavy even in dry weather.

- *The anointing will take authority over your situations.* "For there the Lord commanded the *blessing*" (see Ps. 133:3b).

- *The anointing will lift burdens from your shoulder* (see Isa. 10:27a).

- *The anointing will take away yokes.* They will remove the shackles that have caused you to say and do things and go places you really didn't desire (see Isa. 10:27).

- *The anointing will destroy the yoke.* It isn't enough to just lift the yoke from your neck. If you leave a yoke enabled, it can resume its previous position at any time. The anointing dismantles everything that satan had planned for your life.

In the days of the judges, the Philistines stole the ark of the covenant. They placed the ark beside their god Dagon. The presence of God in the ark caused Dagon to fall on his face. After the Philistines sat him up again, the presence of God caused Dagon to fall a second time. On his second fall, his head was cut off, and also both palms (see I Sam. 5:1-4).

Everything satan planned to do (his head) and all the things he wanted to do (his hands) has been destroyed by the anointing. He has been cut off and rendered helpless.

> *No weapon that is formed against thee shall prosper; and every tongue that shall rise against thee in judgment thou shalt condemn. This is the heritage of the servants of the Lord, and their righteousness is of me, saith the Lord* (Isaiah 54:17).

This level of anointing is vital because we will need to have high-level talks with God that we do not want satan to hear or to understand. We need the ability to change languages. Tongues are available, and they are for you. You can speak the language as the Spirit of God gives the utterance.

The Master Key

As long as we operate according to human logic and our carnal perceptions of things, we will find ourselves up and down with our circumstances. But when we tap into the Holy Ghost, our knowledge takes on a whole new perspective and we begin to operate in Kingdom authority.

We no longer fret when the gates of hell rise up against us because we know that Jesus has given us the master key, which is the anointing of the Holy Ghost. You don't have to worry about being locked in or locked out if you have the master key. The master key can open any lock.

Jesus told Peter not to worry about the gates of hell because He would give him the keys to the Kingdom (see Matt. 16:17-19). These keys were a mystery to others, but to Peter the keys solved any dilemma because they were Kingdom keys. They were a message of prevailing authority to those who understand the code.

Jesus faced these four dilemmas:

1. Traditions of men (see Matt. 15:1-3).

2. Outward religion that left the heart desperately wicked (see Matt. 15:10-20).

3. Physical infirmities, a type of spiritual handicaps (see Matt. 15:29-31).

4. Physical hunger, a type of spiritual starvation and famine (see Matt. 15:32-39).

Jesus asked His disciples, *"Whom do men say that I the Son of man am?"* (Matt. 16:13). Understanding the answer to this question opened the way to an anointing that left the gates of hell powerless.

They answered, *"Some say that thou art John the Baptist: some, Elias; and others, Jeremias, or one of the prophets"* (Matt. 16:14). These were merely fleshly men with limitations.

Then Jesus asked, *"But whom say ye that I am?"* (Matt. 16:15). Peter confessed, *"Thou art the Christ, the Son of the living God"* (Matt. 16:16). The Greek word is *Christos*, the anointed one from God.

Jesus knew these four types of crises had left the people in hopeless situations. They were trying to handle these four areas by seeing Jesus as just an earthly man, a teacher, or a prophet. These four dilemmas had left them victims locked in a prison without a key.

When we recognize Jesus as the Christ, however, He gives us a master key (the anointing) to unlock any crisis in our life. The anointing does not promise to keep the gates of hell from coming against you, but it prevents the gates of hell from prevailing against you.

Everything Has a Price

When you shop, you know that everything has a price tag. As you peruse the merchandise in stores, you probably ask yourself four basic questions:

1. Do I need this particular item?

2. Can I afford the price?

3. Does it have a warranty with it?

4. Would I use it if I bought it?

The anointing falls under these same four guidelines:

1. You desperately need the anointing of the Holy Ghost.

2. The Holy Ghost is well worth the price.

3. The Holy Ghost has a warranty sealed unto the day of redemption.

4. In order to fulfill everything that a sovereign God has ordained for your life, you must use the power of the Holy Ghost to reach your potential and destiny.

Jesus Christ knew the importance of being anointed for works of service. He quoted the prophet Isaiah at the outset of His ministry:

The Spirit of the Lord God is upon me; because the Lord hath anointed me to preach good tidings unto the meek; he hath sent me to bind up the brokenhearted, to proclaim liberty to the captives, and the opening of the prison to them that are bound; to proclaim the acceptable year of the Lord, and the day of vengeance of our God; to comfort all who mourn; to appoint unto them that mourn in Zion, to give unto them beauty for ashes, the oil of joy for mourning, the garment of praise for the spirit of heaviness; that they might be called trees of righteousness, the planting of the Lord, that he might be glorified (Isaiah 61:1-3).

May we cry out for an infilling of the Holy Ghost that we might be enabled to pray in the Spirit and walk in a greater anointing. Like our Master, may we be anointed *"with the Holy Ghost and with power"* (Acts 10:38).

Points to Ponder

The Holy Spirit is your strongest ally.

Spirit praying separates you from worldly pressures.

Praying in the Spirit brings peace.

The anointing brings power.

Tap into the Holy Ghost for wisdom.

We must communicate with God.

Your prayers are like stealth bombers bypassing satan's detection.

We cannot understand the language of God in our own intellect.

The anointing renders satan powerless.

The Holy Ghost pleads God's will to us.

Call down fire from Heaven!

Thoughts and Reflections

_____

_____

_____

_____

_____

_____

_____

_____

_____

_____

_____

_____

_____

Chapter 2

ASK, SEEK, KNOCK

One of the greatest controversies in the entire Bible concerns the Godhead: *"Hear, O Israel: The Lord our God is one Lord"* (Deut. 6:4).

If there is one God, as Scripture teaches, how can there be a Son who says that He and His Father are one? If there is only one God, how can there be *"three that bear record in heaven, the Father, the Word, and the Holy Ghost: and these three are one"* (I John 5:7)?

The concept of the Godhead is a mystery that has baffled Christians for years. With our limited minds we try to comprehend a limitless God. How can we explain one God but three distinct manifestations? Some have used the analogy of ice, water, and steam being the same in substance but differing according to temperature. Others have shown how one man can be a father, a husband, and a son at the same time.

Although we may never completely understand the Godhead, Scripture teaches that our lives can be tremendously impacted by the ministry of the Holy Ghost. The first step is welcoming, or receiving, the power of the Holy Ghost.

You Can Receive the Holy Ghost

You have the right to receive the Holy Ghost because Jesus prayed for you to receive Him: *"And I will pray the Father, and He shall give you another Comforter, that He may abide with you forever"* (John 14:16).

The Greek word for Comforter, *parakletos*, means "one called alongside to help, to defend as an attorney." It also means "another one just like me." The same word means "advocate" in this Scripture: *"My little children, these things write I unto you, that ye sin not. And if any man sin, we have an advocate with the Father, Jesus Christ the righteous"* (1 John 2:1). Christ is our advocate in Heaven; the Holy Ghost is our advocate on earth.

The Holy Ghost has been given to assist us in a variety of ways. He helps to guide us:

Howbeit when He, the Spirit of truth, is come, He will guide you into all truth: for He shall not speak of Himself; but whatsoever He shall hear, that shall He speak: and He will shew you things to come (John 16:13).

He assures us that we are children of God:

The Spirit itself beareth witness with our spirit, that we are the children of God (Romans 8:16).

He gives us power to witness:

But ye shall receive power, after that the Holy Ghost is come upon you: and ye shall be witnesses unto me both in Jerusalem, and in all Judea, and in Samaria, and unto the uttermost part of the earth (Acts 1:8).

He helps us to pray:

Likewise the Spirit also helpeth our infirmities: for we know not what we should pray for as we ought: but the Spirit itself maketh intercession for us with groanings which cannot be uttered (Romans 8:26).

He enables us to bear the fruit of the Spirit:

But the fruit of the Spirit is love, joy, peace, longsuffering, gentleness, goodness, faith, meekness, temperance: against such there is no law (Galatians 5:22-23).

The Holy Ghost is always present. He is our backup!

While Jesus was departing, He prayed that another One just like Him would come. That One is the Holy Ghost. The Holy Ghost would stand by the children of God to assist them in carrying out the same work—and even "greater works:"

Verily, verily, I say unto you, He that believeth on me, the works that I do shall he do also; and greater works than these shall he do; because I go unto my Father (John 14:12).

Believers must understand the ministry of the Holy Ghost so they can carry out the will of God for their lives.

We aren't alone when we lie down at night or go through the storms of life. When we go through a valley or through a trial, the Holy Ghost is there to defend us. God will never leave us nor forsake us (see Heb. 13:5). Jesus is with us to the end of this age (see Matt. 28:20). When we receive the fullness of the Holy Ghost, we receive an eternal friend. Jesus is praying that you have an intimate relationship with the Holy Ghost.

Many friends stay with us until we mess up or until we disagree with them. They quickly leave as if they never knew us. But the Holy Ghost, our Comforter, stays with us forever.

The Holy Ghost does not come and go based on the circumstances of our lives. He is there when we do well; He is there when we fail. When we are on top of things, He is there. When things are on top of us, He is there. No matter what the situation, the Holy Ghost is always there to help us. In the same way that Jesus helped the disciples, the Holy Ghost now helps us.

When Do We Receive the Holy Ghost?

This controversial question has been debated for years. God's Word shows that a person receives the Holy Ghost as a mark of identity, confirming that he or she really is a child of God (see John 3:5-6; Rom. 8:9,14-16; Gal. 4:6). Jesus told His disciples that the world (unbelievers) could not receive the Holy Ghost because it *"seeth Him not"* (John 14:17).

Scripture also shows us, however, that receiving the Holy Ghost at salvation is not the same as being filled with the Holy Ghost. Some disciples followed Jesus for years and only later were filled with the Holy Ghost and spoke with other tongues as the Spirit gave them utterance.

And, behold, I send the promise of my Father upon you: but tarry ye in the city of Jerusalem, until ye be endued with power from on high (Luke 24:49).

In the last day, that great day of the feast, Jesus stood and cried, saying, If any man thirst, let him come unto me, and drink. He that believeth on me, as the scripture hath said, out of his belly shall flow rivers of living water. But this spake He of the Spirit, which they that believe on Him should receive: for the Holy Ghost was not yet given; because that Jesus was not yet glorified (John 7:37-39).

Therefore being by the right hand of God exalted, and having received of the Father the promise of the Holy Ghost, He hath shed forth this, which ye now see and hear. For David is not ascended into the heavens: but he saith himself, The Lord said unto my Lord, Sit thou on my right hand, Until I make thy foes thy footstool. Therefore let all the house of Israel know assuredly, that God hath made that same Jesus, whom ye have crucified, both Lord and Christ. Now when they heard this, they were pricked in their heart, and said unto Peter and to the rest of the apostles, Men and brethren, what shall we do? Then Peter said unto them, Repent, and be baptized every one of you in the name of Jesus Christ for the remission of sins, and ye shall receive the gift of the Holy Ghost. For the promise is unto you, and to your children, and to all that are afar off, even as many as the Lord our God shall call (Acts 2:33-39).

And we are his witnesses of these things; and so is also the Holy Ghost, whom God hath given to them that obey Him (Acts 5:32).

Christ hath redeemed us from the curse of the law, being made a curse for us: for it is written, Cursed is every one that hangeth on a tree: That the blessing of Abraham might come on the Gentiles through Jesus Christ; that we might receive the promise of the Spirit through faith (Galatians 3:13-14).

You can be saved, but not necessarily filled or baptized with the Holy Ghost. We receive the Holy Ghost as a mark of identity when we are saved, but another experience—the baptism in the Holy Ghost—awaits us.

While Peter yet spake these words, the Holy Ghost fell on all them which heard the word. And they of the circumcision which believed were aston- ished, as many as came with Peter, because that on the Gentiles also was poured out the gift of the Holy Ghost. For they heard them speak with tongues, and magnify God (Acts 10:44-46).

And it came to pass, that, while Apollos was at Corinth, Paul having passed through the upper coasts came to Ephesus: and finding certain disciples, He said unto them, Have ye received the Holy Ghost since ye believed? And they said unto him, We have not so much as heard whether there be any Holy Ghost. And he said unto them, Unto what then were ye baptized? And they said, Unto John's baptism. Then said Paul, John verily baptized with the baptism of repentance, saying unto the people, that they should believe on him which should come after him, that is, on Christ Jesus. When they heard this, they were baptized in the name of the Lord Jesus. And when Paul had laid his hands upon them, the Holy Ghost came on them; and they spake with tongues, and prophesied. And all the men were about twelve (Acts 19:1-7).

The believers in these verses had not been baptized in or received the infilling of the Holy Ghost.

The apostle Paul commanded the Ephesian believers to *"be filled with the Spirit"* (Eph. 5:18). They had already been saved by the grace of God (see Eph. 2:8-9) and had been sealed by the Holy Ghost (see Eph. 1:13). They had been positionally placed in the heavenlies with Christ Jesus (see Eph. 2:6). They had become His workmanship (see Eph. 2:10). They had been blessed with every spiritual blessing, chosen before the foundation of the world, and predestined to be adopted by Jesus Christ (see Eph. 1:3-5).

Despite all these things, apostle Paul admonished them to be filled with the Holy Ghost. He did not merely suggest that the saints receive the infilling of the Holy Ghost; he commanded them to do so!

To make his point, the apostle Paul issued two commandments: *"Be not drunk with wine"* and *"Be filled with the Spirit"* (Eph. 5:18). He used a negative command, something we should *not* do, to accentuate something that we should do.

Being "drunk with wine" means that we are intoxicated or under the control of wine. To be drunk means that you have given yourself over to the alcohol. In order to remain drunk, one must continue to partake of whatever brought about the drunkenness.

Paul knew the saints would never come to church or attempt any type of service for the Lord while under the influence of wine. But if it would be wrong to be drunk on wine and attempt to serve God, then it would be equally wrong to attempt to serve God and not be filled or intoxicated with the Holy Ghost.

When a person is drunk, he or she becomes a totally different person. Drunks become very bold, even fearless, as their emotions are overtaken by the wine. Their speech is often slurred, and their walk is unsteady. In order for the Ephesians to be happy and bold, to walk in the will of God, to talk in a new way, and not be afraid of their future, they needed to be filled with the Holy Ghost.

Next, apostle Paul focused on the home, dealing with the relationship between husbands and wives and between parents and their children.

Ephesians closes with a discussion of the battle that we face as children of God. If we are to partake of the blessings that God has predestined for us; if we are to be the workmanship of God; if we are to enjoy a happy marriage and rear children in the fear and admonition of the Lord—then we will face a spiritual battle. Living a Spirit-filled life, however, abundantly equips us to carry out these tasks.

Passover Must Precede Pentecost

The nation of Israel recognized many feasts, but we will only focus on Passover and Pentecost. While these two feasts were primarily for Israel, we can make some dynamic secondary applications for the church.

Passover had been recognized by the Israelites since their departure from the land of Egypt. God commanded the elders of the nation of Israel to kill a lamb and apply its blood to the two side posts and the overhead lintel of the door of every house. That night, God sent a death angel throughout Egypt to slay the firstborn of every household. When He saw the blood over the doorposts of the Israelites, however, He promised to *pass over* them and not execute the same judgment that befell the Egyptians (see Exod. 12).

This is a type of Jesus, who is our Passover Lamb (see I Cor. 5:7). Through His death and shed blood, we have been accepted by God. Seeing the blood of Christ, our substitute, God has passed over us and withheld judgment for our sins.

The time lapse between Passover and Pentecost is significant. Pentecost, which began 50 days after the Passover, marked the beginning of the ingathering of the harvest of the nation of Israel. The people went into their fields to gather the fruit and various grains. Pentecost was also called *"the feast of weeks"* (Exod. 34:22), *"the feast of harvest"* (Exod. 23:16), and *"the day of the firstfruits"* (Num. 28:26).

According to Leviticus 23:22, the harvest had three parts:

1. The main harvest, which consisted of the majority of the harvest.

2. The corners of each field.

3. The gleanings or what was left over, which God commanded the Israelites to leave for the poor and strangers.

This parallels what Jesus told His disciples in Acts 1:8. He mentioned three parts to the disciples' evangelistic ministry:

1. Jerusalem (the main harvest).

2. Judea and Samaria (the corners of the field).

3. The uttermost parts of the earth (the house of Cornelius, the Gentiles, and the strangers).

At Pentecost, believers received power to gather in their harvest, beginning with Jerusalem, then Judea and Samaria, then to the uttermost parts of the earth. This fulfilled Old Testament prophecy concerning Pentecost.

Jesus fulfilled our Passover and lifted judgment from the world (see John 1:29; I Cor. 5:7). He stayed on earth 40 days and then was taken up into Heaven. The Holy Ghost did not come until after Passover. Jesus, our Passover Lamb, ushered in Pentecost.

Some people have been erroneously taught that they were not saved until they received the Holy Ghost and spoke with other tongues. Jesus never said that. Jesus said, *"Even the Spirit of truth; whom the world cannot receive, because it seeth him not, neither knoweth him..."* (John 14:17).

In the same way that Passover preceded Pentecost, we must first have an experience with Jesus, allowing His blood to cleanse us from sin; then we become candidates for the baptism of the Holy Ghost.

Jesus said the Holy Ghost was dwelling *with* the disciples, but after Pentecost the Holy Ghost would be in the disciples. Jesus said, *"For he dwelleth with you, and shall be in you"* (John 14:17). First, though, they had to experience Passover—the blood of Jesus. Then they would experience Pentecost—the power of the Holy Ghost.

A Worthy Candidate for Pentecost

Before He ascended into Heaven, Jesus commanded His disciples to tarry for the promise of the Holy Ghost: *"Behold, I send the promise of my Father upon you: but tarry ye in the city of Jerusalem, until ye be endued with power from on high"* (Luke 24:49).

They had to wait only because the Holy Ghost was making His debut. Now that He has come, however, those who experience a Passover by accepting Jesus Christ, God's Passover Lamb, can receive the baptism of the Holy Ghost.

Many people have not received the Holy Ghost because they feel unworthy. If your own worthiness were the issue, you wouldn't have anything from God. The Christian life is founded on grace from beginning to end.

God does not see you as you are, but He sees you through the blood of Jesus. When Jesus died on the cross, you died with Him. God reckons you to be dead with Christ. *Reckon* means "to figure in something, to write it down, to document it, to take inventory." Although you did not die physically, document your death with Christ, because God sees you in Him when He died.

That's why you must have a Passover before you can have a Pentecost. Passover makes you a worthy and fit candidate for Pentecost. Passover applies the blood to the doors of your heart. The two side posts and top lintel of a doorway form a cross, which is a type of our coming through the cross of Jesus.

Gaining proper standing with God always requires the death of a substitute. God shed the blood of an innocent animal and clothed Adam and Eve with its skins after the fall (see Gen. 3:21). Each Israelite household in Egypt killed an innocent lamb to mark their doors with its blood (see Exod. 12:3-7). Years later, it took the blood of a sinless, innocent man to atone for sin.

> *The next day John seeth Jesus coming unto him, and saith, Behold the Lamb of God, which taketh away the sin of the world* (John 1:29).

> *But God commendeth His love toward us, in that, while we were yet sinners, Christ died for us. Much more then, being now justified by His blood, we shall be saved from wrath through Him* (Romans 5:8-9).

In each of these cases, an individual, a household, and the world could not live up to the standards of a holy God. Only the death of a substitute gave the individual, the household, and the world the standing that God demands.

Every area of your life has been put under the blood of Jesus. He has become your atonement, which means a covering, to put away or to cancel. It also means to reconcile and to make at one with.

God says you are worthy to receive the baptism of the Holy Ghost. Jesus has prayed for you to receive the Comforter. Is it based on your merit? Of course not. You never have and never will live up to the expectations of a holy God. Jesus, who *"ever liveth to make intercession"* (Heb. 7:25), prays confidently because He died in your stead.

Easier Than You Think

Many have made the baptism of the Holy Ghost and the Spirit-filled life so difficult when actually it is quite simple. Many have taught that if you wait long enough, if you pray hard enough, if you lift your hands, sell out, hold on or hold out, that you will receive the Holy Ghost. Although their intentions may be good, their approach is not scriptural.

We can conclude three things regarding receiving the Holy Ghost:

1. Jesus is praying for you to receive.

2. You must experience a Passover before you can receive.

3. If you have had a Passover, you're a worthy candidate to receive the power of Pentecost.

If you have these three things working for you—the prayers of Jesus, the pleading of the blood in His Passover, and anticipation for the power of Pentecost—you are a worthy candidate.

It Begins With a Desire

And I say unto you, Ask, and it shall be given you; seek, and ye shall find; knock, and it shall be opened unto you. For every one that asketh receiveth; and he that seeketh findeth; and to him that knocketh it shall be opened (Luke 11:9-10).

Jesus began His discourse on receiving the Holy Spirit by using a simple three-letter word—ask. When you ask for something, it implies that you desire it: *"Blessed are they which do hunger and thirst after righteousness: for they shall be filled"* (Matt. 5:6).

Notice two words: *hunger* and *thirst*, which imply a desire, a longing, an expectation, a want or a need. God always keeps His children in some type of need so He can meet that need. He always wants us dependent on Him.

Being hungry or thirsty implies that you are in need, and it causes you to ask. God is always attentive to the cries of His children. Jesus simply said, "Ask. I know you are hungry and thirsty. I have what you need. Just ask." Asking implies that you both need and want.

The Lord is my shepherd; I shall not want (Psalm 23:1).

But my God shall supply all your need according to his riches in glory by Christ Jesus (Philippians 4:19).

God will not let your needs and wants go unattended, especially when you desire to be more like Him.

We Must Seek What We Ask For

Jesus said that those who seek shall find. Seek means to desire. Jesus wants us to desire the Holy Ghost. Would you ask someone for something and have your head or hand turned the other way? Jesus wants our hearts to be lined up with what our lips are saying.

God rewards those who diligently seek Him (see Heb. 11:6). *Diligently* means to be stretched out for that which you are asking. It means to crave as an expectant mother craves unusual foods. Nothing else satisfies her except the specific combination she asks for.

The Holy Ghost, His power, and the change that He alone can bring in your life must be so precious that you will not accept a counterfeit. Nothing else will suffice. Is your heart focused with a desire that will not take no for an answer? Do you really want the power of the Holy Ghost?

Jesus taught the parable of the lost coin:

Either what woman having ten pieces of silver, if she lose one piece, doth not light a candle, and sweep the house, and seek diligently till she find it? And when she hath found it, she calleth her friends and her neighbours together, saying, Rejoice with me; for I have found the piece which I had lost (Luke 15:8-9).

When this woman realized she didn't have her precious coin, she lit a candle, swept the house, and searched diligently until she found it. We must be in the same place of earnest seeking in regard to the Holy Ghost.

Upon realizing that we don't have the fullness of the Holy Ghost, we light a candle. The psalmist wrote, *"The entrance of thy words giveth light"* (Ps. 119:130).

We must sweep our house, which means we purge ourselves of anything that isn't of God. Then we must seek the Holy Ghost diligently. We must earnestly want the Holy Ghost and refuse to compromise. You can be real and have the Holy Ghost. It isn't something mysterious. This is God's will for your life!

Learning in Retrospect

Behold, I go forward, but He is not there; and backward, but I cannot perceive Him: on the left hand, where He doth work, but I cannot behold Him; He hideth Himself on the right hand, that I cannot see Him (Job 23:8-9).

There are times when it is difficult to understand God's methods. There are moments when discerning His will is a frustrating endeavor. Perhaps we have these moments because we haven't been given all the information we need to ascertain His ways, as well as His acts. Many times we learn more in retrospect than we do while in the thick of the struggle.

I can look over my shoulder at my past and see that the hand of the Lord has been on me all my life. Yet there were times when I felt completely alone and afraid. Even Jesus once cried out, "'*Eli, Eli, lama sabachthani?' That is to say, 'My God, My God, why hast Thou forsaken Me?'*" (Matt. 27:46b). Suspended on the cross with a bloody, beaten body, He was questioning the acts of God—but He never questioned His relationship with Him. Jesus says in essence, "I don't understand why, but You are still My God!"

Generally we see the workings of God when we look back, but while in the throes of the rumbling winds of life, we are often in search of the Lord. Perhaps we are at our best when we are searching for Him; we have no independence, just raw need. There's no dawdling around with things that have no help or healing. Those are the times we know are jobs for God. If He doesn't help us, we will die.

The search for God is an equal-opportunity experience for all Christians. Regardless of how successful you may be, you will always have times when you just need to find Him. Consecration is the conjoined twin of sanctification. They are born together and are connected. You can't be consecrated to, without being sanctified from. Sanctification sets you apart from distractions, and consecration takes that separated person and quenches his thirst in the presence of the Lord!

> *As the hart panteth after the water brooks, so panteth my soul after Thee, O God. My soul thirsteth for God, for the living God: when shall I come and appear before God? My tears have been my meat day and night, while they continually say unto me, Where is thy God? When I remember these things, I pour out my soul in me: for I had gone with the multitude, I went with them to the house of God, with the voice of joy and praise, with a multitude that kept holyday* (Psalm 42:1-4).

The search for God is a primary step into worship. We never search for anything we don't value. The very fact that we search for Him indicates that He has become essential to us. There are millions of people who seem to live their lives without noticing that something is missing. They seemingly sense no real void. Our separating ourselves from these ranks and saying, "God, I need You," is a form of worship. The word *worship* stems from the term "worth-ship." It expresses the worth of an object. The kind of intensity that causes an individual to pursue the invisible in spite of all the visible distractions is a result of need. If we didn't need Him desperately, we could easily be satisfied with carnal things.

Hide-and-Seek

God instructs us to seek Him, but not as though He were hiding from us. He is not a child playing hide-and-seek. He isn't crouched behind trees, giggling while we suffer. The request to seek Him is as much for our benefit as His. When we seek Him, we make a conscious decision that is necessary for bringing us into the realm of the spiritual. The pursuit of God is rewarding in the development of the seeker's character. Some levels of blessings are never received unless they are diligently sought. It is this seeking after God that often propels Him to perform. If that were not true, the woman with the issue of blood would never have been healed (see Matt. 9:19-21). Her conscious decision to seek the impossible released the invisible virtue of God.

But without faith it is impossible to please Him: for he that cometh to God must believe that He is, and that He is a rewarder of them that diligently seek Him (Hebrews 11:6).

There are no manuals that instruct us step by step as to the proper way to seek the Lord. Like lovemaking, the pursuit is spontaneous and individually conceived out of the power of the moment. Some seek Him quietly, with soft tears falling quietly down a weary face. Others seek Him while walking the sandy beaches of a cove, gazing into the swelling currents of an evening tide. Some raise their hands and praise Him with loving expressions of adoration. There are no rules—just that we seek Him with our whole hearts.

We are like blind people when it comes to spiritual issues; we are limited. However, we should be challenged by our limitations. When there is a strong desire, we overcome our inabilities and press our way into His presence.

My friend, don't be afraid to stretch out your hands to reach after Him. Cry after Him. Whatever you do, do not allow this moment to pass you by!

And hath made of one blood all nations of men for to dwell on all the face of the earth, and hath determined the times before appointed, and the bounds of their habitation; that they should seek the Lord, if haply they might feel after Him, and find Him, though He be not far from every one of us (Acts 17:26-27).

Like groping fingers extended in the night trying to compensate for a darkened vision, we feel after God. We feel after His will and His ways. I'm amazed at all the people who seem to always know everything God is saying about everything. In the hymn, *My Faith Looks Up to Thee*, Ray Palmer and Lowell Mason wrote, "My faith looks up to thee, Oh lamb of Calvary, Savior divine." On the one hand, my faith looks up because my eyes can't always see. On the other hand, there is a healthy reaction that occurs in blindness; our senses become keener as we exercise areas that we wouldn't normally need.

God knows what it will take to bring us to a place of searching. He knows how to stir us from our tranquil and comfortable perching position of supremacy. There are times when even our great sages of this age murmur in the night. When the congregants have gone home and the crowd dissipates, there are moments in which even our most profound, articulate leaders grope in the dark for the plan and purpose of God. In spite of our strong gait and stiff backs, in spite of our rigid posture and swelling speech, behind the scenes we tremble in our hearts at the presence of God whose sovereign will often escape the realm of our human reasoning.

All-Points Bulletin

Searching releases answers. The Word declares, "*Seek, and ye shall find*" (Matt. 7:7b). Many things available to us will not be found without an all-out search. Seeking God also takes focus. This search has to be what the police call an *APB*. What does that mean? An APB is an "all-points bulletin." All of the departments are asked to seek the same thing. Thus, our search can't be a distracted, half-hearted curiosity. There must be something to produce a unified effort to seek God. Body, soul, and spirit—all points—must be seeking the same thing. There is a blessing waiting for us. It will require an APB to bring it into existence, but it will be worth attaining. Who knows what God will release if we go on an all-out God-hunt?

I believe there are times when we grow weary of human answers. The crucial times that arise in our lives require more than good advice. We need a word from God. There are moments when we need total seclusion. We come home from work, take the telephone receiver off the hook, close the blinds, and lie before God for a closer connection.

In Job's case, he was going through an absolute crisis. His finances were obliterated. His cattle, donkeys, and oxen were destroyed. His crops were gone. In those days, it would be comparable to a stock market crash, taking all of his hard-won money with it. It was as if Job, the richest man, had gone bankrupt. What a shock to his system to realize how vulnerable he was. It is sobering to realize that one incident, or a sequence of events, can radically alter our lifestyles.

Unfortunately, it generally takes devastation on a business level to make most people commit more of their interest in relationships. Job probably could have reached out to his children for comfort, but he had lost them, too. His marriage had deteriorated to the degree that Job said his wife abhorred his breath (see Job 19:17). Then he also became ill.

Have you ever gone through a time in your life when you felt you had been jinxed? Everything that could go wrong, did! Frustration turned into alienation. What do you do when a crisis hits, making you feel imprisoned? Do you use this moment to seek God, or to brood over your misfortune? With the right answer, you could turn your jail into a church!

> *Seek ye the Lord while He may be found, call ye upon Him while He is near: let the wicked forsake his way, and the unrighteous man his thoughts: and let him return unto the Lord, and He will have mercy upon him; and to our God, for He will abundantly pardon (Isaiah 55:6-7).*

Job said, "*Behold, I go forward, but He is not there*" (Job 23:8a). It is terrifying when you see no change coming in the future. Comfort comes when you know that the current adversity will soon be over. But what comfort can be found when it seems the problem will never cease? Like a rainstorm that will not cease, the waters of discouragement begin to fill your tossing ship with water. Suddenly you experience a sinking feeling. However, there is no way to sink a ship when you do not allow the waters from the outside to get on the inside! If the storm keeps coming, the lightning continues to flash, and the thunder thumps on through the night, what matters is keeping the waters out of the inside. Keep that stuff out of your spirit!

How many persons needlessly died because they struggled in the water and finally drowned? We say they drowned because they couldn't swim. The real truth is, many times, they drowned because they couldn't trust! If they had relaxed, the same current that drummed them down would have lifted them up so they could float. It isn't always the circumstance that is so damaging to us; it is our reaction to the circumstances. The hysterical flailing and gasping of desperation causes us to become submerged beneath the currents of what will soon pass if we can keep our wits about us.

Left Hand

Have you been searching and seeking and yet feel that you are getting no closer? Perhaps you are closer than you think. Here is a clue that may end your search. Job told us where to find Him. He told us where He works. If you were looking for someone and you knew where he worked, you wouldn't have to search very long. Job said that God works on the left hand (see Job 23:9)!

I know you've been looking on the right hand, and I can understand why. The right hand in the Bible symbolizes power and authority. That's why Christ is seated on the right side of God (see Mark 16:19). Whenever you say someone is your right hand, you mean he is next in command or authority. *Right hand* means power. Naturally, then, if you were to search for God, you would look on the right hand. Granted, He is on the right hand. He is full of authority. But you forgot something. His strength is made perfect in weakness (see 2 Cor. 12:9). He displays His glory in the ashes of human frailty. He works on the left hand!

Let me present my daughter Cora as an illustration. When she was born, her mother and I noticed that she learned to hold her bottle in her right hand. We naturally assumed that she was *right-handed*. However, to our surprise, when she grew a little older she held her cup in her left hand. To this day there are certain things she does with her right hand and certain things she does with her left. Technically, they call it ambidexterity. Cora is what my grandmother would call even-handed. The hand she uses depends on what she is trying to accomplish. Cora is ambidextrous. So is God! He is simply ambidextrous. There are times He will move on the left side.

Listen for God's hammering in the spirit. You can't see Him when He's working on the left side; He is invisible over there. It appears that He is not there, but He is.

You Have to Knock!

Those who want the power of the Holy Ghost must take a three-step approach: *ask, seek,* and *knock.* What prompts you to open your front door? When someone knocks, you see who it is and what they want.

Jesus said to knock. Before knocking, you must have a desire to ask. This driving desire caused you to come to the door with great expectation and determination. You searched until you found the door, and having found it, you knock.

It may seem that Jesus has these steps out of order, but that's not true. If you have no will to ask, there's no reason to knock. Without the will to seek, there's no reason to knock. Knocking is preceded by a will to ask and search diligently. Knocking gives you access to what you have diligently sought.

How Much More...

An earthly father can be very biased. Sometimes he is stubborn, and sometimes he gives for all the wrong reasons. Jesus made it very clear: If the child asks for one thing, the Father will not give another. He then asked a question: *"If ye then, being evil, know how to give good gifts unto your children:* **how much more** *shall your heavenly Father give the Holy Spirit to them that ask him?"* (Luke 11:13). The emphasis is on *"how much more."*

God knows that we need the power of the Holy Ghost. Spiritual gifts function only as the Holy Ghost empowers the child of God. As you ask and seek, remember that God knows your motives. He endues you with the power of the Holy Ghost to give you victory over satan, to make you joyful, and to enable you to function in the gifts of the Spirit.

Take the Word as authoritative—ask, seek, knock. Be like the woman who had lost her precious coin. She wanted it so badly that she searched with a candle and swept her house clean.

The Power of the Holy Ghost

Old Testament types have their fulfillment in the New Testament. Daniel wrote about a fourth man in the fiery furnace with the three Hebrew children; Moses spoke of the rock that followed the children of Israel; each Israelite household killed a lamb for its Passover. All of these were types of Christ.

The Holy Ghost is likened to wind or breath.

The wind bloweth where it listeth, and thou hearest the sound thereof, but canst not tell whence it cometh, and whither it goeth: so is every one that is born of the Spirit (John 3:8).

And suddenly there came a sound from Heaven as of a rushing mighty wind, and it filled all the house where they were sitting (Acts 2:2).

The power of the Holy Ghost can make you everything God said you could be. Adam illustrates this perfectly. The Bible says that Adam was only a form until God breathed on him (see Gen. 2:7). Only then did Adam become a living soul.

Until then, he had potential but no power. When God breathed into Adam, he received the power to reach his potential. The mere form of man became a living soul. The word *living* means to be vibrant, alive, and strong. You have great potential in your life. With great potential comes great responsibility. God has shaped you, but you need power to become everything He desires for you to become. Without the power of the Holy Ghost you can go to Heaven, but you will never reach your potential. Your ministry, your gifts, your calling, your life, and your marriage will be only a form of what it could have been.

An Exceedingly Great Army

Without a word from God, without the energizing breath of the Holy Ghost, you are only a mere form of what you can be. This is similar to the valley of dry bones that Ezekiel saw. Before the prophet lay a potential army, but without the Word of the Lord they were merely a form of what they could have been.

Let's look at five principles we can learn from Ezekiel 37:

1. You must be willing to confess your condition. *"They were very dry"* (vs. 2).

2. You must confess that you are merely a form of what you could be.

- The valley was *"full of bones"* (vs. 1).

- The structure of an army was just waiting for God's command.

3. You must hear the Word of God. *"Prophesy upon these bones, and say unto them, O ye dry bones, hear the word of the Lord"* (vs. 4).

- The anointing only falls upon truth. God will not put His seal of approval on something until He is sure that it is His.

- The Word brings the truth that ultimately sets us free (see John 8:32).

4. The Word will bring about change.

- The dry bones heard and were quickened (vs. 4).

- They heard their potential. *"I will cause breath to enter into you, and ye shall live"* (vs. 5).

- They knew they were not complete at this stage. *"I will lay sinews upon you, and will bring flesh upon you, and cover you with skin"* (vs. 6). The Word brought about a noise as broken pieces began to come together (vs. 7). God will speak to your broken and shattered dreams.

- The Word brought a shaking (vs. 7). We need to be shaken out of our complacency, tradition, formalism, and doctrines.

- The Word formed real people with arms, legs, eyes, and feet. They were still not complete, however. *"But there was no breath in them"* (vs. 8).

5. The potential will be realized as the Word brings about the wind. *"Prophesy unto the wind, prophesy, son of man, and say to the wind, Thus saith the Lord God; Come from the four winds, O breath, and breathe upon these slain, that they may live"* (vs. 9).

The wind gave potential, the ability to carry out what they were capable of doing. The Word came from the four corners of the earth. That tells me there isn't an area that God cannot fill with the Holy Ghost—your past, your childhood, your feelings of inferiority, your wounds, your loneliness. The Holy Ghost can fill you from the north, south, east, and west.

This pile of bones had a potential that Ezekiel couldn't see, just as you have unseen potential. No matter what others say, God sees incredible potential in you. The Word of God says you're capable. Within you is an army. You merely need to dispel satan's fear and allow the wind to breathe upon that which God has formed in you.

Points to Ponder

The Holy Ghost is our backup!

The Comforter is always with us.

Saints are commanded to receive the infilling of the Holy Ghost.

Christian life is founded on grace.

Ask!

Seek!

Knock!

Searching for God brings out our best.

Seek Him with your whole heart.

Trust!

Reach your potential with power from the Holy Ghost.

Within you is an army.

Thoughts and Reflections

_____

_____

_____

_____

_____

_____

_____

_____

_____

_____

_____

_____

_____

Chapter 3

TONGUES OF FIRE AND THE REFINER'S FIRE

B efore the day of Pentecost, the Holy Ghost had come upon men and women periodically, usually to empower them for specific tasks given by God as portrayed in the Old Testament. Pentecost fulfilled Old Testament prophecy and many predictions made by Jesus Himself.

Christ taught His disciples to pray, "*Thy Kingdom come*" (Matt. 6:10). The apostle Paul said, "*The Kingdom of God is not meat and drink* [it was not by observing any particular feast, custom, or ritual]; *but righteousness, and peace, and joy in the Holy Ghost*" (Rom. 14:17).

The Holy Ghost came as the authority and power of the Kingdom of God. The disciples had witnessed the miracles of Jesus. They saw His death and burial. They also saw the resurrected Christ stand in their presence three days later, which amazed them. Even Thomas, who was a doubter, stood in awe and declared, "*My Lord and my God!*" (John 20:28).

Even though they had seen and testified to this, the disciples could not just go on their way preaching. Jesus had given them specific instructions: *"Tarry ye in the city of Jerusalem, until ye be endued with power from on high"* (Luke 24:49).

God wanted a witness from Heaven to empower humankind: "Only an earthen vessel empowered from Heaven could declare the glories of the world to come."

The doctrine of speaking in tongues and being baptized in the Holy Ghost has been accompanied by much controversy. Let's turn to the Scriptures to look at the initial outpouring of the Holy Ghost.

> *And when the day of Pentecost was fully come, they were all with one accord in one place. And suddenly there came a sound from Heaven as of a rushing mighty wind, and it filled all the house where they were sitting. And there appeared unto them cloven tongues like as of fire, and it sat upon each of them. And they were all filled with the Holy Ghost, and began to speak with other tongues, as the Spirit gave them utterance* (Acts 2:1-4).

What happened on the day of Pentecost?

1. This event came right on time. *"And when the day of Pentecost was fully come..."* (vs. 1).

2. A sound from heaven, like a rushing mighty wind, filled all the house where they were sitting (vs. 2).

3. *"...tongues...of fire...sat upon each of them"* (vs. 3).

4. They *"were all filled with the Holy Ghost, and began to speak with other tongues"* (vs. 4).

5. The language came *"as the Spirit gave them utterance"* (vs. 4b).

Pentecost Has Fully Come

The Jewish people were familiar with the term *Pentecost*. Everything God did in types and shadows in the Old Testament was fulfilled in the New Testament. In the Old Testament, God revealed Himself in many ways to Israel. He was known as the "I Am," promising to sustain them on their journey from Egypt to Canaan. Whatever they needed, He was the I Am of sustenance for that very thing.

One word gives us an understanding of this concept—the word *true*. Jesus said, *"My Father giveth you the true bread from heaven"* (John 6:32).

True means "to have without concealment." Throughout the Old Testament, God had been concealed in type and shadow. In the New Testament, however, He is no longer concealed. He became in reality everything that He merely was a shadow of in the Old Testament.

Pentecost was a type of something that one day would explode and change this world for eternity. *Pentecost* meant "fiftieth day." When we read, "The day of Pentecost had fully come," it means the fiftieth day after Passover had arrived.

Everything that needed to precede this memorable day had taken place. Jesus, the Passover Lamb, had died and risen from the dead. He had walked with His disciples, was confirmed 40 days and nights with many infallible proofs, and then was received into glory.

Our personal Passover must precede our Pentecost. The blood of Christ prepares us for Pentecost, washing away our sin and prejudice, enabling us to come together with devout men and women from every nation. You cannot have a Pentecost with God if you are biased against people—not just racial prejudice but experiential prejudice. People have devised a grading scale between one and ten for the severity of certain sins. Sin, which simply means to miss the mark, has no scale of severity in the eyes of God.

God is tearing down racial, ethnic, and religious barriers, bringing people together from all walks of life in one place with one focus: to reach the world for Jesus. We need it to be said of us, "The day of Pentecost has fully come." The word *fully* means "to come with an expected end, to come with anticipation, to come to have a part in a mission."

Pentecost marked the beginning of a mission for the Jewish people as they gathered in the fruit of their labors. Pentecost in Acts 2 marked the beginning of a mission for the church to gather in lost souls. We need Pentecost to fully arise in our life as we fall in love with Jesus, the Passover Lamb, to carry out the ingathering of His harvest.

The Sound Filled the House

The sound from Heaven "filled all the house where they were sitting." This sound was a sign, witnessing that Heaven was speaking. The Greek word for sound denotes a loud rumbling or roaring voice, much like the rumbling of a tornado that precedes the storm.

This wind filled closets, bedrooms, upstairs, and downstairs. It filled all the components in the house: jars, glasses, significant and insignificant things. This indicates that anyone can be filled with the Holy Ghost.

We have seen saved Baptists, Methodists, Catholics—all walks of Christian professions—filled with the Holy Ghost with the evidence of speaking with other tongues. The only mandatory prerequisite is that you be a believer—a born-again, blood-washed child of God (see Acts 2:38,39; John 14:17).

What about the place where you are sitting? What about your home church? Is it filled with the Holy Ghost? Has your assembly experienced a Pentecost that is filling everything inside? A person becomes a product of his environment. You will begin to resemble whatever you are around—good or bad.

Tongues of Fire Sat on Each One

This experience was not for a select few. The cloven tongues of fire rested on each one—men and women, young and old, apostles and disciples. Hearing the sound, the amazed multitude asked, "What do these things mean?" Apostle Peter stood and said:

> *This is that which was spoken by the prophet Joel; And it shall come to pass in the last days, saith God, I will pour out of my Spirit upon all flesh: and your sons and your daughters shall prophesy, and your young*

men shall see visions, and your old men shall dream dreams: And on my servants and on my handmaidens I will pour out in those days of my Spirit; and they shall prophesy (Acts 2:16-18).

God planned for His Spirit, a consuming fire, to rest upon each of His children. Apostle Peter told the crowd, *"For the promise is unto you, and to your children, and to all that are afar off, even as many as the Lord our God shall call "* (Acts 2:39).

Peter, who later preached to the Gentiles in Cornelius' house, said, *"Of a truth I perceive that God is no respecter of persons"* (Acts 10:34). He saw the Holy Spirit fall on the assembly even before he finished his sermon, confirming God's promise.

They Spoke with Other Tongues

They *"began to speak with other tongues"* (Acts 2:4). Tongues in this passage is the Greek word *glossary*, which simply means "a language."

Devout Jews from every nation had gathered in Jerusalem for Pentecost. When the Holy Spirit was poured out and the disciples began to speak in tongues, it caused quite a stir.

Now when this was noised abroad, the multitude came together, and were confounded, because that every man heard them speak in his own language. And they were all amazed and marvelled, saying one to another, Behold, are not all these which speak Galilaeans? And how hear we every man in our own tongue, wherein we were born? Parthians, and Medes, and Elamites, and the dwellers in Mesopotamia, and in Judaea, and Cappadocia, in Pontus, and Asia, Phrygia, and Pamphylia, in Egypt, and in the parts of Libya about Cyrene, and the strangers of Rome, Jews and proselytes, Cretes and Arabians, we do hear them speak in our tongues the wonderful works of God (Acts 2:6-11).

Luke mentions over a dozen locations in this passage, representing many languages and dialects. Tongues enabled the multitude to hear the mighty deeds of God in their own language.

The Spirit Gave Them Utterance

The language came *"as the Spirit gave them utterance"* (Acts 2:4). Utterance means the ability to speak plainly, to declare openly, or to have the ability to enunciate with clarity. The people spoke, but the words came through the ability or enabling of the Holy Ghost. They spoke as the Spirit gave utterance.

When you do something, you are doing it with assistance. If you walk across the room, you are walking as your feet move. Your feet are the tools being used to carry out the mission of walking. Suppose you fly to Chicago. It could be said that you traveled to Chicago as the plane flew, meaning that you flew by the auspice of the plane.

The believers at Pentecost spoke the language of Heaven, but only as the Holy Ghost gave them utterance.

God Gave a Pattern

As mentioned previously, the Old Testament conveys many truths concealed in types and shadows. Everything the Old

Testament tabernacle depicted in some type or shadow the glory of God in the face of Jesus Christ. The tabernacle was not an idea imagined by Moses. As God gave him the blueprint, Moses built it after the pattern he saw in Heaven (see Exod. 25:8-40).

> *Moses was admonished of God when he was about to make the tabernacle: for, See, saith he, that thou make all things according to the pattern shewed to thee in the mount* (Hebrews 8:5).

Moses merely built what Heaven had envisioned. Tongues are no different than a pattern.

As Moses was commanded to build by the pattern, so we are to speak by the pattern as the Spirit gives utterance. Tongues come because the Spirit gives the utterance or the ability to speak or enunciate.

People with hearing problems almost always have a speech impediment. Our ability to hear gives us the ability to articulate or enunciate. Without hearing, we are limited in our ability to speak. The same is true in the Spirit.

We must hear before we can speak. At Pentecost, they heard *"a sound from Heaven as of a rushing mighty wind....And they...began to speak with other tongues, as the Spirit gave them utterance"* (Acts 2:2-4). They heard the sound, then they spoke.

God said Israel would not hear Him because of their uncircumcised ears. This simply means they were carnal and fleshly. We must walk in the Spirit to hear the Spirit. To understand the ways of God, we must listen not to human logic but to the One who *"knoweth what is the mind of the Spirit"* (Rom. 8:27).

In the Old Testament, God spoke a pattern of what He wanted to be built on earth. God also used a sound to witness to the Old Testament saints. God hasn't changed His methods for we who live today.

Exodus 28:33-35 describes the design of the high priest's garment. On the hem of his garment were pomegranates of blue, purple, and scarlet, symbolizing freshness of life, royalty, and the blood. A golden bell was fastened on either side of the fruit for a sign to the people. When the high priest went into the holy place to minister as mediator, he took blood and offered it upon the mercy seat. The people could not see him, but if they heard the golden bells they knew the sacrifice had been accepted and the priest lived. This sound was a sign for the people that their sins had been atoned for.

After the resurrection of Christ, He showed Himself to the disciples and others for 40 days. Before ascending to Heaven, Jesus told His followers to wait for the promise of the Father. They gathered for prayer and waited as Christ took up the office of high priest forever.

The Jews knew that the Passover resulted in the death of an innocent lamb. Fifty days later marked the beginning of their harvest or the feast of ingathering. Jesus said He was the Passover Lamb. Pentecost marked 50 days since His blood had been poured out for the forgiveness of sins.

The disciples' wait ended. *"And when the day of Pentecost was fully come...there came a sound..."* (Acts 2:1-2). This was the fulfillment of the pomegranates and golden bells. The bells were a sign that the sacrifice had been accepted, and the Holy Ghost was the sound that our sins had been atoned for.

Have Tongues Ceased?

Charity never faileth: but whether there be prophecies, they shall fail; whether there be tongues, they shall cease; whether there be knowledge, it shall vanish away. For we know in part, and we prophesy in part. But when that which is perfect is come, then that which is in part shall be done away" (I Corinthians 13:8-10).

Many denominations have interpreted this verse to mean that spiritual gifts, including tongues, have ceased. But is this theory accurate?

They say "that which is perfect" is the complete, written Scriptures. If this is the case, then knowledge is also done away with—and we know that isn't true. By putting the verse in context, tongues, prophecies, and knowledge still exist because "that which is perfect" (the second coming of Christ) has not yet taken place.

The gifts of the Spirit enable us to see a glimpse of His glory, but we still *"know in part, and we prophesy in part"* (I Cor. 13:9). The shadow, the images, the glimpse of His glory, will pale in comparison to Christ Himself when He reigns in glory. The gifts help us and attend to many of our needs. But when we see Jesus face to face, we will graduate from gifts, which are only a glimpse, to the giver—Jesus Christ Himself.

No matter how spiritual we become, no matter how much Greek and Hebrew we may learn, and no matter how much we pray and study, our understanding of God at its best is only partial. Apostle Paul wrote, *"For now we see through a glass, darkly; but then face to face: now I know in part; but then shall I know even as also I am known*" (I Cor. 13:12). Until then, however, tongues continue for the use and edification of the believer.

Why Tongues?

God chose tongues as a sign for a significant reason. We can understand His sovereign selection of tongues from this passage:

> *For in many things we offend all. If any man offend not in word, the same is a perfect man, and able also to bridle the whole body. Behold, we put bits in the horses' mouths, that they may obey us; and we turn about their whole body. Behold also the ships, which though they be so great, and are driven of fierce winds, yet are they turned about with a very small helm, withersoever the governor listeth. Even so the tongue is a little member, and boasteth great things. Behold, how great a matter a little fire kindleth! And the tongue is a fire, a world of iniquity: so is the tongue among our members, that it defileth the whole body, and setteth on fire the course of nature; and it is set on fire of hell. For every kind of beasts, and of birds, and of serpents, and of things in the sea, is tamed, and hath been tamed of mankind: but the tongue can no man tame; it is an unruly evil, full of deadly poison* (James 3:2-8).

Let's summarize some of these truths:

- Every beast and animal has been tamed by humankind, except the tongue.

- If we can control the tongue, we can control the whole body.

- Very large things can be controlled by something very small.

- The tongue is a fire.

God often employs natural examples to bring about spiritual understanding. Jesus often used natural, physical, tangible analogies in His parables. He talked about a man who sowed seed, a woman who searched for a lost coin, and servants who invested their master's money to describe the Kingdom of God.

In this passage, God uses the tongue to teach truth. The tongue is a fire—something out of control, something that is difficult if not impossible to tame. If we can control the tongue, this enables us to control every aspect of our lives.

James pointed out that something very large can be guided by something very small. A horse can be controlled by the bit in its mouth. James knew that a horse wasn't tamed by chaining its feet or wrapping something around its neck. A horse can be guided by controlling its movements from the mouth. Likewise, a large ship can be guided across rough waters with little effort by using a small wheel—the helm—that guides the ship and controls its direction.

When we are filled with the Holy Ghost, He acts as a deterrent. He places a bit in our mouths and bridles our speech. Just when you feel like telling someone off, the Holy Ghost takes control. Isn't it exciting that God took the tongue, a member of our body known for being "a fire, a world of iniquity," and sanctified it for His purposes?

When God filled the disciples on the day of Pentecost, He sent tongues of fire to sit on each of them. God caused them to speak with a heavenly language, proving He had control of these believers.

Why did God choose tongues as a sign? He took the most difficult, uncontrollable member of our body and caused it to yield to divinely inspired speech. Bridling the tongue may be impossible for us to do in our own strength, but the supernatural outpouring of the Holy Ghost enabled the disciples to use their tongues for the purposes of God—and it will do the same for us.

Two Types of Tongues

Speaking in tongues can occur in two different settings. A believer may pray in tongues privately to commune with God:

For he that speaketh in an unknown tongue speaketh not unto men, but unto God: for no man understandeth him; howbeit in the spirit he speaketh mysteries....He that speaketh in an unknown tongue edifieth himself (1 Corinthians 14:2,4).

Scripture also teaches on the gift of tongues or "divers [different] kinds of tongues."

First Corinthians 12:10, which is used in a public assembly. Apostle Paul gave instructions on regulating this gift: "*If any man speak in an unknown tongue, let it be by two, or at the most by three, and that by course; and let one interpret*" (1 Cor. 14:27).

Without the interpretation of tongues, the church will not be edified.

I would that ye all spake with tongues, but rather that ye prophesied: for greater is he that prophesieth that he that speaketh with tongues, except he interpret, that the church may receive edifying (I Corinthians 14:5).

We also find the phrase *"to one is given"* (I Cor. 12:8), which implies that not all will have the same gift any more than members of a body have the same functions.

A body has many members, yet their functions differ from each other. The hand cannot function as a foot, or vice versa. In the same way, the Spirit gives different gifts to different people.

We also find in First Corinthians 12:4-7 four important truths:

1. Gifts come by the Spirit (vs. 4).

2. Each gift has a different administration (vs. 5).

3. Each gift has a different operation (vs. 6).

4. Gifts are given *"to every man to profit withal"* (vs. 7). The gifts of the Spirit are always manifested to minister and help people, never to cause harm, confusion, or division.

There is a difference between the gift of tongues and tongues used as a prayer language. The gift of tongues benefits the hearers; the prayer language benefits only the speaker. If you fail to understand the difference between speaking in tongues and the gift of tongues, you have missed the whole issue and will become con-fused. As a result, you may even confuse others.

When the gift of tongues is given in a public assembly, the message needs to be interpreted for the hearers to benefit. Sometimes, however, such as on the day of Pentecost, the gift of tongues is given to minister to the hearers in their own language (see Acts 2:6).

For example, suppose you were in Russia and the Holy Spirit enabled you to speak fluent Russian. This miraculous sign would cause the people to understand in their own language and it would be a witness and a confirmation of the gift itself.

In the law it is written, With men of other tongues and other lips will I speak unto this people; and yet for all that will they not hear me, saith the Lord. Wherefore tongues are for a sign, not to them that believe, but to them that believe not: but prophesying serveth not for them that believe not, but for them which believe (I Corinthians 14:21-22).

God said that He would speak to men in other tongues and with other lips, "yet for all that will they not hear me." Isn't it amazing that men can see the gift of God in operation and hear the manifestation of the Holy Ghost but fail to believe? Mockers concluded, *"These men are full of new wine"* (Acts 2:13).

Being filled with the Holy Ghost, however, gives us tremen-dous power for living the Christian life.

Empowerment Not Entertainment

The Holy Ghost has not been given to the Church to entertain congregations but rather to empower them. Jesus said, *"Ye shall receive power, after that the Holy Ghost is come upon you"* (Acts 1:8). The Holy Ghost gives us power not to just shout, run the aisles, or to put on a show. He empowers us to intervene in society as a witness.

Jesus gave these instructions to His disciples:

And these signs shall follow them that believe; In my name they shall cast out devils; they shall speak with new tongues; they shall take up serpents; and if they drink any deadly thing, it shall not hurt them; they shall lay hands on the sick, and they shall recover (Mark 16:17-18).

The Book of Acts records the amazing signs and wonders that occurred through the disciples. What was the catalyst for these miracles? Pentecost. After being endued with power from on high, *"they went forth, and preached everywhere, the Lord working with them, and confirming the word with signs following"* (Mark 16:20).

That's the kind of power we need to transform our lives, families, churches, and society. To that end, the Refiner uses His fire to purify His creation allowing the vessel to become all that He intends it to be.

The Refiner's Fire

We often face discouragement in this world. Many have never had anyone who believed in them. Even after achieving some level of success in one area or another, many have not had anyone to point out their potential. Isn't it amazing how we can see so much potential in others, yet find it difficult to unlock our own hidden treasure? Highly motivated people are not exempt from needing someone to underline their strengths and weaknesses. Nurturing is the investment necessary to stimulate the potential that we possess. Without nurturing, inner strengths may remain dormant. Therefore, it is crucial to our development that there be some degree of nurturing the intrinsic resources we possess.

There is a difference in the emotional makeup of a child who has had a substantial deposit of affection and affirmation. Great affirmation occurs when someone invests into our personhood. I believe that people are the greatest investments in the world. A wonderful bond exists between the person who invests and the one in whom the investment is made.

Although it is true that fire will not destroy gold, it is important to note that fire purifies the gold. When God gets ready to polish His gold, he uses fiery trials. Unfortunately, nothing brings luster to your character and commitment to your heart like opposition does. The finished product is a result of the fiery process. Whenever you see someone shining with the kind of brilliancy that enables God to look down and see Himself, you are looking at someone who has been through the furnace of affliction.

Let me warn you: God places His prize possessions in the fire. The previous vessels that He draws the most brilliant glory from often are exposed to the melting pot of distress. The bad news is, even those who live godly lives will suffer persecution. The good news is, you might be in the fire, but God controls the thermostat! He knows how hot it needs to be to accomplish His purpose in your life. I don't know anyone I would rather trust with the thermostat than the God of all grace.

Every test has degrees. Some people have experienced similar distresses, but to varying degrees. God knows the temperature that will burn away the impurities from His purpose. It is sad to have to admit this, but many times we release the ungodliness from our lives only as we experience the dread chastisement of a faithful God who is committed to bringing about change. How often He has had to fan the flames around me to produce the effects that He wanted in my life! In short, God is serious about producing the change in our lives that will glorify Him.

I indeed baptize you with water unto repentance: but He that cometh after me is mightier than I, whose shoes I am not worthy to bear: He shall baptize you with the Holy Ghost, and with fire: Whose fan is in His hand, and He will thoroughly purge His floor, and gather His wheat into the garner; but He will burn up the chaff with unquenchable fire (Matthew 3:11-12).

His hand has fanned the flames that were needed to teach patience, prayer, and many other invaluable lessons. We need His correction. We don't enjoy them, but we need them. Without the correction of the Lord, we continue in our own way. What a joy to know that He cares enough to straighten out the jagged places in our lives. It is His fatherly corrections that confirm us as legitimate sons—not illegitimate ones. He affirms my position in Him by correcting and chastening me.

But if ye be with chastisement, whereof all are partakers, then are ye bastards, and not sons (Hebrews 12:8).

It is impossible to discuss the value of investing in people and not find ourselves worshiping God—what a perfect picture of investment. God is the major stockholder. No matter whom He later uses to enhance our characters, we need to remember the magnitude of God's investment in our lives. The greatest primary investment He made was the inflated, unthinkable price of redemption that He paid. No one else would have bought us at that price. He paid the ultimate price when He died for our sins. What He did on the Cross was worship. According to *Nelson's Bible Dictionary*, the word worship, literally translated, means "to express the worth of an object." Normally, the lesser worships the greater, but this time, the greater worshiped the lesser. What an investment!

His Investment

Explore with me the concept that God has an investment in our lives. First of all, no one invests without the expectation of gain. What would a perfect God have to gain from investing in imperfect humanity? The apostle Paul wrote, *"But we have this treasure in earthen vessels, that the excellency of the power may be of God, and not of us"* (2 Cor. 4:7). Thus, according to Scripture, we possess treasure. However, the excellency of what we have is not of us, but of God. The treasure is of God. That implies that this treasure originates from God. It is accumulated in us and then presented back to Him.

No farmer plants a field in the ground because he wants more earth. No, his expectation is in the seed that he planted. The ground is just the environment for the planted seed. The seed is the farmer's investment. The harvest is his return, or more accurately, his inheritance as the outer encasement of the seed dies in the ground. Harvest cost the seed its life. Jesus said, *"Verily, verily, I say unto you, Except a corn of wheat fall into the ground and die, it abideth alone: but if it die, it bringeth forth much fruit"* (John 12:24).

We are that fertile ground—broken by troubles, enriched by failures, and watered with tears. Yet undeniably there is a deposit within us. This deposit is valuable enough to place us on satan's hit list. In writing to the Ephesian church, Paul prayed that *"the eyes of your understanding being enlightened..."* (Eph. 1:18). One of the things he wanted the people to know is the riches of His inheritance in the saints! Paul challenged them to become progressively aware of the enormity of His inheritance in us, not our inheritance in Him. We spend most of our time talking about what we want from God. The real issue is what He wants from us. It is the Lord who has the greatest investment. We are the parched, dry ground from which Christ springs. Believe me, God is serious about His investment!

To the enemy the Lord says, *"Touch not Mine anointed, and do My prophets no harm"* (1 Chron. 16:22). God will fight to protect the investment He has placed in your life. What a comfort it is to know that the Lord has a vested interest in my deliverance. He has more than just concern for me. God has begun the necessary process of cultivating what He has invested in my life. Have you ever stopped to think that it was God's divine purpose that kept you afloat when others capsized beneath the load of life? Look at

Job; he knew that God had an investment in his life that no season of distress could eradicate: *"But He knoweth the way that I take: when He hath tried me, I shall come forth as gold"* (Job 23:10).

Remember the story of the three Hebrew boys in the fiery furnace? When the wicked king placed them in the fire, he thought the fire would burn them. He didn't know that when you belong to God, the fire only burns the ties that bind you. People have said that God took the heat out of the furnace. That is not true. Consider the soldiers who threw the Hebrews into the fire—they were burned to death at the door! There was plenty of heat in the furnace. God, however, controls the boundaries. Have you ever gone through a dilemma that should have scorched every area of your life and yet you survived the pressure? Then you ought to know that He is Lord over the fire!

It has been suggested that if you walk in the Spirit, you won't have to contend with the fire. Real faith doesn't mean you won't go through the fire, however. Real faith simply means that when you pass through the fire, He will be with you. This thought brings you to an unusual reality. In most cases, if I told you that tomorrow you would be burned alive, but not to worry because I would be in the fire with you, my presence in the dilemma would provide no comfort at all. Yet the presence of the Lord can turn a burning inferno into a walk in the park! The Bible says a fourth person was in the fire, and so the three Hebrews were able to walk around unharmed in it (see Dan. 3).

King Nebuchadnezzar was astonished when he saw them overcome what had destroyed other men. I cannot guarantee that you will not face terrifying situations if you believe God. I can declare that if you face them with Christ's presence, the effects of the circumstance will be drastically altered. It is quite popular to suggest that faith prohibits trouble. But when I read about these young Hebrew men, I realize that if you believe God, you can walk in what other men burn in. Seldom will anyone fully appreciate the fire you have walked through, but be assured that God knows the fiery path to accomplishment. He can heal the blistered feet of the traveler.

Hear God, See His Works

When John was on the isle of Patmos, he was limited to a cave but free in his spirit (see Rev. 1). Remember, satan may work feverishly to limit the ministry and reputation of God's vessel, but he can never confine the anointing and the call on your life. Every ministry gift will eventually confront the cave of loneliness and the prison of an ostracized situation. Nevertheless, let the jailer beware; our God has a prison ministry. He explodes the walls of impossibility.

John wrote that he heard the thunderous voice of the Lord. In the process of seeking the voice, he encountered seven golden candlesticks (vs. 12). The candlesticks are later revealed as the Church. We need men and women who hear the voice of God before they see the work of God. What good will it do us to polish the candelabra and light the candles if there is no voice of God to cause people to turn aside and see?

When the voice of God led to the presence of Christ, John collapsed in the presence of the Lord. A deluge flooded the cave as Christ opened His mouth; His voice sounded as the noise of many waters. John said that many waters were in His voice, but the fire was on His feet. Effective communication is always trans-mitted from the base of burned feet. John said Jesus' feet looked as if they had been in the fire. What a comfort to the indicated character of this Pentecost preacher to find that the feet of his Consoler had been through the fire. Dearly beloved, hear me today: Your Deliverer has feet that have been burned. He knows what it feels like to be in the fire.

Thank God for the smoldering feet of our Lord that run swiftly to meet His children in need.

But still the question remains, "Is there any preventative pro-tection that will at least aid the victim who struggles in the throes of a fiery test?" If you are in a fiery trial, be advised that it is your faith that is on trial. If you are to overcome the dilemma, it will not be by your feelings, but by your faith. In First John 5:4, Jesus says, "*For whatsoever is born of God overcometh the world: and this is the victory that overcometh the world, even our faith.*" Yes, it is the shield of faith that quenches the fiery darts of the devil (see Eph. 6:16).

The term *quench* means "to extinguish." Are there any fires brewing that you would like to extinguish? Your faith will do the job. If faith doesn't deliver you *from* it, then it will surely deliver you *through* it.

The fanaticism of some faith theology has intimidated many Christians from faith concepts as they relate to the promises of God. Yet faith is such a key issue for the Christian that the peo-ple of the early Church were simply called *believers* in recognition of their great faith. One thing we need to do is understand the distinctions of faith. Faith cannot alter purpose; it only acts as an agent to assist in fulfilling the predetermined purpose of God. If God's plan requires that we suffer certain opposition in order to *accomplish* His purpose, then faith becomes the vehicle that enables us to persevere and delivers us through the test.

On the other hand, the enemy afflicts the believer in an attempt to *abort* the purpose of God. Faith is a night watchman sent to guide the purpose of God. It will deliver us out of the hand of the enemy—the enemy being anything that hinders the purpose of God in our lives.

> *From that time on Jesus began to explain to His disciples that He must go to Jerusalem and suffer many things at the hands of the elders, chief priests and teachers of the law, and that He must be killed and on the third day be raised to life. Peter took Him aside and began to rebuke Him. "Never, Lord!" he said. "This shall never happen to You!" Jesus turned and said to Peter, "Get behind Me, Satan! You are a stumbling block to me; you do not have in mind the things of God, but the things of men"* (Matthew 16:21-23 NIV).

Faith

Hebrews chapter 11 discusses at length the definition of faith. It then shares the deeds of faith in verses 32-35a, and finally, it discusses the perseverance of faith in verses 35b-39.

There are distinctions of faith as well. In Hebrews 11:32-35a, the teaching has placed an intensified kind of emphasis on the distinct faith that escapes peril and overcomes obstacles: "*Quenched the violence of fire, escaped the edge of the sword, out of weakness were made strong, waxed valiant in fight, turned to flight the armies of the aliens*" (Heb. 11:34).

However, in the verses that end the chapter, almost as if they were footnotes, the writer deals with the distinctions of another kind of faith. In his closing remarks, he shares that there were some other believers whose faith was exemplified *through* suffering and not *from* suffering.

And others had trial of cruel mockings and scourgings, yea, moreover of bonds and imprisonment: They were stoned, they were sawn asunder, were tempted, were slain with the sword: they wandered about in sheepskins and goatskins; being destitute, afflicted, tormented (Hebrews 11:36-37).

Christianity's foundation is not built on elite mansions, stocks and bonds, or sports cars and cruise-control living. All these things are wonderful if God chooses to bless you with them. However, to make finances the symbol of our faith is ridiculous. The Church is built on the backs of men and women who withstood discomfort for a cause. These people were not the end but the means whereby God was glorified. Some of them exhibited their faith through their shadows' healing sick people. Still others exhibited their faith by bleeding to death beneath piles of stone. They also had a brand of faith that seemed to ease the effect, though it didn't alter the cause.

As the fire of persecution forces us to make deeper levels of commitment, it is so important that our faith be renewed to match our level of commitment. There is a place in God where the fire consumes every other desire but to know the Lord in the power of His resurrection. At this level, all other pursuits tarnish and seem worthless in comparison. Perhaps this is what Paul really pressed toward, that place of total surrender. Certainly that is the place I reach toward, which often escapes my grasp, but never my view. Like a child standing on his toes, I reach after a place too high to be touched. My hands are extended, my feet are on fire—and I listen for His voice!

Points to Ponder

He is the great I Am.

God is breaking down barriers to reach the world for Jesus.

We must hear before we can speak.

Taming the tongue gives us power to control our lives.

The gift of tongues benefits hearers;
prayer language benefits the speaker.

Inner strengths may remain dormant without nurturing.

His hand fans the flames.

God is serious about His investment.

Satan can never confine the anointing and calling on your life.

Christianity is based on the Church standing firm for Christ.

Thoughts and Reflections

_____

_____

_____

_____

_____

_____

_____

_____

_____

_____

_____

_____

_____

_____

Chapter 4

SECRET CODE

G od has spoken to His people from the very beginning:

> *And they heard the voice of the Lord God walking in the garden in the cool of the day: and Adam and his wife hid themselves from the presence of the Lord God amongst the trees of the garden* (Genesis 3:8).

He communicated His desire for them to keep the garden, to be fruitful and multiply, and not to eat of the tree of the knowledge of good and evil.

God spoke to His people through the prophets:

> *God, who at sundry times and in divers manners spake in time past unto the fathers by the prophets* (Hebrews I:I).

He also spoke to us by His Son:

God...hath in these last days spoken unto us by his Son, whom he hath appointed heir of all things, by whom also he made the worlds (Hebrews 1:1-2).

He spoke to us by miracles:

God also bearing them witness, both with signs and wonders, and with divers miracles, and gifts of the Holy Ghost, according to his own will (Hebrews 2:4).

He then spoke by His apostles. As a result of the mighty out-pouring at Pentecost, God said He would speak through His Spirit.

And it shall come to pass afterward, that I will pour out my spirit upon all flesh; and your sons and your daughters shall prophesy, your old men shall dream dreams, your young men shall see visions (Joel 2:28).

Many try to limit God, saying He has spoken in the past but has ceased to speak today. This, however, is not true. God continues to speak to us through His written Word.

The Holy Ghost also speaks to us today. Tongues are God's message for the last days. It isn't the only way that He can speak, but it is one avenue of speech. We need faith to allow Him to speak and interpret the message through a willing vessel.

The issue in biblical times and today is this: Can you hear what God is saying? God is certainly speaking:

He that hath an ear, let him hear what the Spirit saith unto the churches; He that overcometh shall not be hurt of the second death (Revelation 2:11).

Howbeit when he, the Spirit of truth, is come, he will guide you into all truth: for he shall not speak of himself; but whatsoever he shall hear, that shall he speak: and he will shew you things to come (John 16:13).

We need to get hold of God like never before because He is speaking a vital message in these last days. He is looking for someone to deliver a timely, life-changing word. Many times, however, it is in secret code and can only be understood by those who have the Holy Ghost.

Surely the Lord God will do nothing, but he revealeth his secret unto his servants the prophets (Amos 3:7).

The secret things belong unto the Lord our God: but those things which are revealed belong unto us and to our children for ever, that we may do all the words of this law (Deuteronomy 29:29).

But when the children of Israel cried unto the Lord, the Lord raised them up a deliverer, Ehud the son of Gera, a Benjamite, a man left-handed: and by him the children of Israel sent a present unto Eglon the king of Moab.... But he himself turned again from the quarries that were by Gilgal, and said, I have a secret errand unto thee, O king (Judges 3:15,19).

These three passages show us some interesting things:

1. God has some secrets (see Deut. 29:29).

2. He reveals these secrets to His servants (see Amos 3:7).

3. God looks for willing servants to deliver these secret messages (see Judg. 3:19).

Every message has four components:

1. A person who sends the message.

2. A person who receives the message.

3. A third party who may be involved because the person sending the message cannot always contact the primary party directly. In this case, he or she contacts someone who will deliver the message.

4. The interpretation of the message conveys what is meant by the person sending it. The message must be made plain and spoken in a way that can be understood.

Why Secret Code?

Why should God speak in secret code, and to whom is He speaking? When God speaks in secret, He does so for at least two reasons:

1. God wants to have an intimate relationship with you. You tell your secrets and innermost thoughts only to your closest, most trusted friends.

2. By speaking in secret code, God ensures that the devil does not understand the strategy of the church. This enables us to make an unannounced surprise attack because the secret code bypasses the radar and defense system of the satanic forces in opposition to us (see Eph. 6:12).

Mysteries of the Kingdom

If ye love me, keep my commandments. And I will pray the Father, and he shall give you another Comforter, that he may abide with you for ever; Even the Spirit of truth; whom the world cannot receive, because it seeth him not, neither knoweth him: but ye know him; for he dwelleth with you, and shall be in you. I will not leave you comfortless: I will come to you. Yet a little while, and the world seeth me no more; but ye see me: because I live, ye shall live also. At that day ye shall know that I am in my Father, and ye in me, and I in you (John 14:15-20).

This Scripture indicates the Kingdom of God was going through some drastic changes:

- *We find the changing of the guard. "I will pray the Father, and he shall give you another Comforter"* (vs. 16). Another in this passage means another one just like me. Jesus confirmed this in the very next verse: *"Ye know him* [the Spirit of truth]; *for he dwelleth with you, and shall be in you"* (vs. 17).

- *We find an obligation on our part to receive the Holy Ghost.* Jesus said, *"If ye love me, keep my commandments"* (vs. 15). As a result of our walking in obedience, Jesus said that He would pray to the Father. He in turn would send another Comforter to us.

Jesus said three things about the Holy Ghost in John 14:17:

1. The world cannot receive Him.

2. The world cannot see Him, because His ways are not their ways; He is a mystery to them.

3. The world doesn't know Him.

All the miracles of Christ declared what His followers would do in that day. Because the world did not receive Him, did not see Him, and did not know Him, they crucified the Lord of glory.

Only Christ's inner circle of Peter, James, and John witnessed His transfiguration (see Matt. 17:1-9). Only these three saw the inner turmoil of Jesus as He poured out His soul in prayer and conformed to the Father's will in the Garden of Gethsemane (see Matt. 26:37-44).

Only John went to the cross. Is it any wonder that he received an amazing vision known as "The Revelation of Jesus Christ"? Before receiving this vision, he was exiled to the isle of Patmos.

Jesus spoke mysteries to His beloved friend John that still perplex the world—and even the Church. In order to receive this surpassing revelation, John had to detach himself from earthly things. He heard a voice say, *"Come up hither, and I will shew thee things which must be hereafter"* (Rev. 4:1).

God calls those who are committed to excellence to a place of seclusion and aloneness. The Holy Ghost is saying, "Detach yourself from things that blind you from seeing My mysteries and deafen you from hearing My language."

Jesus is speaking, but even those in the Church are missing Him because they do not hear His language. Many are not hearing His voice because tradition has left them content with only the first glimpse of His glory. The glory of Christ far exceeds any glory ever known by man. In those three short years Jesus began to reveal the mysteries of a powerful Kingdom that was greater than any problem, sickness, or dilemma.

They Didn't Understand Him

Why did the people crucify the Prince of Glory? Jesus Christ had a message, power, and authority that frightened the religious hierarchy of His day. Yes, He was a Jew who spoke the regional dialect. But sometimes He also spoke mysteries to His disciples. Thousands followed Christ, but He handpicked 12 to be with Him.

Why aren't more believers hearing from God? Many are not walking in obedience and do not have the fullness of the Holy Ghost. Jesus only reveals His secrets to those who are trustworthy and have intimate fellowship with Him.

Jesus told His disciples that the world would not understand, see, or know, but those who had the Holy Ghost would.

Yet a little while, and the world seeth me no more; but ye see me: because I live, ye shall live also. At that day ye shall know that I am in my Father, and ye in me, and I in you (John 14:19-20).

He was saying, "In that day they will see me as dead, but you will know that I am still in control. When they bury Me in a tomb, some will say it's over. But you will know I spoke mysteries the world could not understand. Destroy this temple and in three days I will raise it up. When they come on that first Easter morning and find My body gone, they will say it was stolen. You will know that I have risen from the dead. My ministry will continue through the Holy Ghost."

"At that day ye shall know" (John 14:20) *denotes something progressive. "Then shall we know, if we follow on to know the Lord"* (Hos. 6:3). *"Ye shall know the truth"* (John 8:32). *"When I became a man"* (I Cor. 13:11) denotes something that isn't complete but is in the making.

Surpassing Our Intellect

Apostle Paul wrote about Kingdom revelation that staggers the mind. The truth is spoken and revealed in secret code. We must understand the code:

But as it is written [in Isa. 64:4], "Eye hath not seen, nor ear heard, neither have entered into the heart of man, the things which God hath prepared for them that love him." But God hath revealed them unto us by his Spirit: for the Spirit searcheth all things, yea, the deep things of God (I Corinthians 2:9-10).

- The code is being spoken. *"But God hath revealed"* (vs. 10a).

- The code speaks *"the deep things of God"*—the mysteries of the Kingdom (vs. 10b).

- The code speaks only to those who have an intimate relationship with God. *"The things which God hath prepared for them that love him"* (vs. 9b).

- The code speaks things that our carnal nature can neither attain nor perceive. Carnality cannot see. *"Eye hath not seen."* Carnality cannot hear. *"Ear hath not heard."* Carnality cannot feel. *"Neither have entered into the heart of man"* (vs. 9a).

A Product of Our Environment

Wherefore, my beloved, as ye have always obeyed, not as in my presence only, but now much more in my absence, work out your own salvation with fear and trembling. For it is God which worketh in you both to will and to do of his good pleasure (Philippians 2:12-13).

This passage of Scripture shows us two things:

1. *Things will begin to work their way out. "Work out your own salvation"* (vs. 12).

2. *The things that work out do so as a result of things working in. "For it is God which worketh in"* (vs. 13). If you stay

around something—be it good or bad—eventually you will begin to resemble it.

Noah's ark looked the same on the outside as on the inside. God told Noah, "...*pitch it within [inside] and without [outside] with pitch*" (Gen. 6:14). Pitch is a sealant. God wants to do a work beginning inside you until it also manifests outwardly in the form of signs.

And these signs shall follow them that believe; In my name shall they cast out devils; they shall speak with new tongues (Mark 16:17).

Jesus wants the church to become so attached to His anointing and so detached from the world that we begin to resemble the Kingdom.

For the Kingdom of God is not meat and drink; but righteousness, and peace, and joy in the Holy Ghost (Romans 14:17).

As the Kingdom of God functions in the mystery of the Holy Ghost, it will become something that far exceeds a group of rituals, traditions, ceremonies, rules, and guidelines.

As we get in tune with the voice of the Spirit, we begin to produce the fruit of the Spirit. The fruit of the Spirit comes from nothing more than the Church falling in love with Jesus and becoming impregnated with His seed (the Word). This will produce the fruit of the Spirit. First, however, we must have an intimate relationship with God.

Do You Know Jesus?

First, do you know Him in the pardon and forgiveness of your sins? Second, do you know Him intimately? Has your relationship with Jesus grown to the point at which you both recognize Him and produce His offspring (the fruit of the Spirit)?

We find this truth throughout Scripture. After creating the first couple, God said, *"Therefore shall a man...cleave unto his wife: and they shall be one flesh"* (Gen. 2:24). Adam and Eve were together and knew each other. *"And Adam knew Eve his wife; and she conceived"* (Gen. 4:1). *"And Cain knew his wife; and she conceived"* (Gen. 4:17). *"And Adam knew his wife again; and she bare a son"* (Gen. 4:25).

After the angel announced to Mary that she had been favored to conceive and bear God's Son, a startled young virgin asked, *"How shall this be, seeing I know not a man?"* (Luke 1:34).

These Scriptures bring out one point: You cannot produce offspring without intimacy. Many Christians have had spiritual orgasms but have never conceived the seed of God's Word. In order for us to bring forth Kingdom offspring, we must know the King of the Kingdom. Jesus said, *"At that day ye shall know that I am in my Father, and ye in me, and I in you"* (John 14:20).

We need to know the Lord Jesus in a spiritually intimate way. The only way to know Him is to be filled with the Holy Ghost. As we walk in what we know, our outward person begins to resemble our inward being.

Light and Salt

As the Church allows the Holy Ghost to work in and through us, the world will begin to see Jesus and the Kingdom of God in action. It will be a mystery to the world but a powerful reality to the Church. But it won't happen overnight. It's progressive, day by day, trial by trial, storm by storm, valley by valley, and temptation by temptation.

When Jesus was on earth, He said, *"I am the light of the world: he that followeth me shall not walk in darkness, but shall have the light of life"* (John 8:12). But when He died, darkness covered the earth. Except for the Holy Ghost, darkness would prevail. However, as the Body of Christ allows the Holy Ghost to fill every fiber of our being, we become the light of the world.

We are a beacon, a lighthouse to a world of storm-tossed, beaten, battered individuals. We are to be a city set on a hill and illuminated by the Holy Ghost. Our joy, our peace, our righteousness should shine brightly, encouraging others to find a refuge in our God. The fruit of the Spirit in our lives will act as a magnet and draw them to Jesus.

Jesus used another analogy for His Church: He called us salt. When Jesus walked the earth, He was a preservative for this world. A thief could not die without first being preserved by His forgiveness (see Luke 23:42); a widow's only son, the apple of her eye, could not reach the gates of death without Jesus stopping the funeral procession (see Luke 7:12). Lazarus could not lay decomposing in a tomb without hearing a voice, *"Lazarus, come forth!"* (John 11:43).

As the Church comes into a Kingdom relationship with Jesus, we then become preservatives:

Ye are the salt of the earth: but if the salt have lost his savour, wherewith shall it be salted? it is thenceforth good for nothing, but to be cast out, and to be trodden under foot of men (Matthew 5:13).

Salt does several things:

1. It creates thirst.

2. It preserves.

3. If poured into wounds, it will burn.

4. If spread by shaking, it will season.

We need to allow the Holy Ghost to saturate our very being so we become sons of God who carry on the Kingdom work.

God Has Your Number

The gift of tongues can be understood by using the telephone as an analogy. One party calls in; the other party receives. This gives you a twofold ability to call sometimes and to hear sometimes.

God is ringing your telephone today. He may have to call you to give you a message for someone else, who for one reason or another cannot hear. The only way the message can get through is for you to speak out what God has spoken into your spirit. Be sure to pray for an interpreter.

God does the calling and you do the receiving. Remember, sometimes certain parties cannot be reached so the caller will contact you to pass on the message. God may call other parties, but for one reason or another they do not hear.

Sometimes they are out of the calling area (too far from God). Sometimes they give God a busy signal (too occupied for God). Sometimes they simply won't answer (too disrespectful toward God). When this happens, God dials your number and gives you a message in a heavenly language that can be interpreted.

Many anointed people wrongly believe that their anointing gives them the right to get out of order. They may exercise their gift, but the message of God is misrepresented, wrong, or even damaging. This confuses and wounds people.

Your anointing does not give you the right to come in and wreck a service: *"And the spirits of the prophets are subject to the prophets"* (I Cor. 14:32).

When a true manifestation of God comes with a message in tongues, we need to pray for the interpretation, which is just as important as the message. Otherwise, how will the people understand? If this does not come, then someone is out of order: *"For God is not the author of confusion, but of peace, as in all churches of the saints"* (I Cor. 14:33).

Timeliness is another important issue with the gift of tongues. Your anointing may not always be in dispute as much as your timing. If your message is not given in its proper timing, it can hurt, confuse, and mislead. The Holy Spirit is not unseemly. He does not cause disorder.

The Corinthian church didn't have a problem with spirituality, but with order. There must be a balance. We need Spirit-filled churches, but we also need Word-filled churches that have the wisdom to know how to function.

Is it any wonder that satan battles the gifts and manifestations of the Holy Ghost? He knows the gifts of the Spirit are going to cause the Church to perform signs, bringing the gospel to our troubled, chaotic society.

God said: *"The people that do know their God shall be strong, and do exploits"* (Dan. 11:32). God is looking for a Church that believes He can confirm them and their ministry with gifts, signs, and wonders in the Holy Ghost (see Heb. 2:3-4 and Mark 16:17-18).

Don't be dismayed if those who see you say, "These people are fanatics!" The Holy Ghost will cause a division between truth and falsehood. When you begin to function in the gift of God for your life and the devil sees a true manifestation of the Holy Ghost, expect to be put on the devil's hit list. This is nothing more than a trick of the enemy to get you to stop.

A God Who Shows Up

In the Old Testament, God would just show up with a message and say, "Let it be," and it was so. God will step in just when you think He won't, just when you need Him, just in time. What was the difference between the God of Elijah and the god of the prophets of Baal? The God of Elijah showed up.

And call ye on the name of your gods, and I will call on the name of the Lord: and the God that answereth by fire, let him be God. And all the people answered and said, It is well spoken (I Kings 18:24).

Now if God appeared on the scene for a prophet who had only the blood of an animal sacrifice, how much more will He appear for those who have the blood of Jesus and the baptism of the Holy Ghost?

Then the king sent unto him a captain of fifty with his fifty. And he went up to him: and, behold, he sat on the top of an hill. And he spake unto him, Thou man of God, the king hath said, Come down (2 Kings 1:9).

When the king sent a captain of 50 to Elijah, he confronted the prophet. Elijah refused to come down:

And Elijah answered and said to the captain of fifty, If I be a man of God, then let fire come down from heaven, and consume thee and thy fifty. And there came down fire from heaven, and consumed him and his fifty (2 Kings 1:10).

The fire of God consumed this messenger and his 50 soldiers, then another captain with his 50 soldiers (vs. 12).

We need to have this same spirit. When tempted to align ourselves with the world, we must tell the devil, "I cannot and will not come down!" All too often people are so close to the devil that they are not intimidating his kingdom at all. But when the Kingdom of light stands in unity, the kingdom of darkness comes down.

And Jesus knew their thoughts, and said unto them, Every kingdom divided against itself is brought to desolation; and every city or house divided against itself shall not stand (Matthew 12:25).

Many church folks have followed the path of society. We live in a fast-food world where nobody wants to wait. Even church people want a quick fix. We want power without pursuing the power giver. But anyone who has ever been mightily anointed of God has had to pursue God.

As the hart panteth after the water brooks, so panteth my soul after thee, O God. My soul thirsteth for God, for the living God: when shall I come and appear before God? (Psalm 42:1-2)

The Holy Ghost Doesn't Speak His Own Agenda

Howbeit when he, the Spirit of truth, is come, he will guide you into all truth: for he shall not speak of himself; but whatsoever he shall hear, that shall he speak: and he will shew you things to come (John 16:13).

This verse, discussed in Chapter 2, gives us some insight regarding the ministry of the Holy Spirit:

- *One day the Holy Spirit would reign in authority.* "When he, the Spirit of truth, is come" signified a day when He would arrive to minister and reign in authority.

- *The Holy Spirit will guide you into all truth.* The ministry of the Holy Spirit involves guidance, but the guidance is the truth of God's Word. Jesus said, *"And ye shall know the truth, and the truth shall make you free"* (John 8:32).

- *The Holy Spirit does not come to fulfill His own agenda.* "For he shall not speak of himself."

- *The Holy Spirit listens before He speaks.* "But whatsoever he shall hear, that shall he speak." The Holy Ghost listens from the portals of glory to hear the will of God. This is why we must listen before we speak as the Holy Spirit gives utterance. The Holy Spirit pleads, with groanings, the will of God for our life.

Sometimes He dials our number to give someone else a message. Have you ever answered the phone and learned the caller wanted to speak to someone else? We usually ask, "Who is this?" and "May I take a message?"

The Holy Spirit may be calling that person, but He isn't getting through. In this case, He may give us a message to relay to the other party. The Holy Ghost hears from Heaven and relays the message to someone who has the gift of tongues. Then we need to pray for someone to take the heavenly language and interpret it to the congregation.

Can You Hear the Holy Ghost?

God is definitely speaking to His people. The question is: Can we hear Him? The Holy Ghost is speaking right now. He is speaking words of truth and guidance. He speaks what He hears in Heaven.

Whenever the Holy Ghost speaks, He testifies that He has been in the boardroom of Heaven. Hearing from Him causes us to lift our head. Just when satan thought he had you, to his amazement you begin to shout. He doesn't know it, but you heard a word.

You may be going through a valley, but the Holy Ghost told you that Jesus is the Lily of the Valley. You may be going down a perplexing path, but you heard that Jesus is a Wonderful Counselor. You may be going through a famine in your life and ministry, but you heard a word that said, "Trust Me when you can't trace Me." You may be facing an insurmountable trial, but you heard a word that said, "Stand still and see the salvation of the Lord."

I heard a word, and you can, too. Sometimes the word is for you, and sometimes it is for someone else. Sometimes God merely wants to use you as a spokesperson.

Jonah's name means "carrier pigeon." God had a message for him to deliver to a third party, the people of Nineveh.

Allow God to use you.

Seven Areas

Has someone ever tried to relay a message to you over the phone? The words they spoke weren't their own, but belonged to someone else. Someone gave them a message, and they, in turn, repeated what they heard.

In the same way the Holy Ghost has you on the line and speaks a word to you. It may not be a word directly from the Bible, but it is a *rhema* word designed to fit your crisis.

Remember that the Holy Ghost doesn't speak on His own initiative. He doesn't convey His own ideas or plans. He speaks only what He hears from Heaven.

Let's look at seven areas of your life in which the Holy Ghost wants to speak:

1. Things beyond human comprehension.

2. Testimony.

3. Direction.

4. Discipline.

5. Companionship.

6. Prioritization.

7. Warning.

Things Beyond Human Comprehension

The Holy Ghost wants to speak to you things that go beyond human logic, natural tendency, and physical comprehension.

But, as it is written, Eye hath not seen, nor ear heard, neither have entered into the heart of man, the things which God hath prepared for them that love him. But God hath revealed them unto us by his Spirit: for the Spirit searcheth all things, yea, the deep things of God (I Corinthians 2:9-10).

In order for us to speak out revelations, we must first allow revelations to be spoken into our spirits.

But the natural man receiveth not the things of the Spirit of God: for they are foolishness unto him: neither can he know them, because they are spiritually discerned (I Corinthians 2:14).

What the Spirit wants to speak and reveal goes beyond three of our five senses.

- *Spiritual revelation goes beyond our seeing. "Eye hath not seen"* (I Cor. 2:9). What God wants to show us cannot be seen through our fleshly eyes.

- *Spiritual revelation goes beyond our ability to hear. "Ear hath not heard"* (I Cor. 2:9). We need a spiritual ear to hear what the Spirit is saying to the church in these last days (see Rev. 2:17).

- *Spiritual revelation goes beyond anything we have ever felt before.* "*Neither have entered into the heart of man*" (I Cor. 2:9). No matter how good we have ever felt in the Spirit, we have never reached the heights that raw spiritual revelation will give. How will you ever persuade people to see, hear, and feel the things of the Spirit if you are not sold on them yourself?

Testimony

The Holy Ghost will testify to you. "*The Spirit itself beareth witness with our spirit, that we are the children of God*" (Rom. 8:16). Notice three things:

1. *There is a testimony.* "The Spirit...beareth witness." This means He testifies as one who stands as an eyewitness to corroborate your statement.

2. *He testifies to our spirit.* He beareth witness "with our spirit." Our innermost being needs a testimony, for it is through our testimony that we overcome the devil.

3. *God doesn't delegate this important task.* "The Spirit itself" speaks regarding our sonship and becoming joint heirs with Christ (see Rom. 8:17). We are His beneficiaries. "*He* [the Holy Ghost] *shall take of mine, and shall shew it unto you*" (John 16:15). He witnesses that we are God's children. Then He shows us what is ours because we're heirs.

Direction

The Holy Ghost will give you direction. Notice what the Spirit said to Philip: *"Go near, and join thyself to this chariot"* (Acts 8:29). Sometimes the message for yourself or others gives direction as to what you should do next.

Discipline

The Holy Ghost speaks to lead us to obedience (see Acts 10:1-23). God gave Peter a vision, telling him not to consider unclean *"what God hath cleansed"* (vs. 15). As Peter pondered a heavenly vision and wondered what it meant, the Holy Spirit spoke to him.

> *While Peter thought on the vision, the Spirit said unto him, Behold, three men seek thee. Arise therefore, and get thee down, and go with them, doubting nothing: for I have sent them* (Acts 10:19-20).

Despite the vision, Peter was not eager to give up his prejudicial disobedience until the Holy Ghost spoke. His words broke down the barriers of racism, religion, and prejudice.

Companionship

The Holy Ghost shows you God's choice for companionship.

As they ministered to the Lord, and fasted, the Holy Ghost said, Separate me Barnabas and Saul for the work whereunto I have called them (Acts 13:2).

This verse focused on two partners in ministry, but the voice of the Holy Spirit can also have an illuminating impact on selecting a partner for marriage or business.

Prioritization

The Holy Ghost will speak and close doors that were the right thing but the wrong time.

Now when they had gone throughout Phrygia and the region of Galatia, and were forbidden of the Holy Ghost to preach the word in Asia, After they were come to Mysia, preach the word in Asia, After they were come to Mysia, they assayed to go into Bithynia: but the Spirit suffered them not (Acts 16:6-7).

Paul and Silas were doing the right thing, but it wasn't timely. Unknown to these apostles, a man was crying out desperately for help in Macedonia. The Holy Ghost prioritized Philippi over Galatia and Bithynia because of the need in one man's life.

Warning

The Holy Ghost sometimes warns us: "*And finding disciples, we tarried there seven days: who said to Paul through the Spirit, that he should not go up to Jerusalem"* (Acts 21:4). If we listen to the warnings of the Holy Ghost, we will avoid many difficulties and snares.

The Holy Ghost speaks for a variety of reasons. His word may be for you or someone else. He may testify to your spirit of God's faithfulness. He may give you direction. He may lead you to obey God's will for your life. He may speak into your spirit His special choice of companionship for marriage, ministry, or business. The Holy Ghost may be trying to close doors that are right but not timely for us. Finally, the Holy Ghost may speak a word of warning.

God is trying to intervene in your life. He may use you to intervene in the life of someone else who may not be answering His call. Whatever the case, you can be confident that it is right because our *parakletos*, the Holy Ghost, only speaks the counsel that He has heard in Heaven.

Not for Prestige

A person who prays in tongues will not get the recognition and commendation of men. It is a very undesirable position. It is a very taxing, laborious position. You are working as hard as, if not harder than, the evangelist or pastor, but you don't receive the praise of men. No, this ministry is obscured and isolated because it is seemingly insignificant.

It is a position that few have ever gotten to and even fewer remain in. Many walk around thrilled that they have the power of the Holy Ghost, but what are they doing with this anointing? God gives this power that we might function in its flow.

One of the greatest blessings ever given to the church was the ability to talk to God on a higher level. God chose to do some of His most intimate communication from a mountain. God took Noah to Mt. Ararat; Abraham to Mt. Moriah; Moses to Mt. Horeb; Joshua to Hebron; Elijah to Mt. Carmel. Jesus told the apostle John to "come up hither" to receive the revelation.

In these last days, God is calling together a Church that has gone beyond playing games. We have pushed our way into the holy of holies, and we're going to see a manifestation of God like never before in the history of the Church.

A secret code is being spoken from Heaven to earth and from earth to Heaven. Men and women will profit by receiving this secret code. As the Holy Ghost speaks through you, ask God to reveal His heart. You will begin to see God's guidance, direction, and comfort in new ways. This will profit you and influence others as you speak out what God has spoken into your spirit.

Points to Ponder

Jesus is speaking—listen.

Open yourself to God's word in you.

Be a beacon for the dark world.

Timeliness is key.

Kingdom light destroys satan's darkness.

Are you listening?

The Holy Ghost speaks for a variety of reasons.

Allow the Holy Ghost to flow through you.

Thoughts and Reflections

_____

_____

_____

_____

_____

_____

_____

_____

_____

_____

_____

_____

Chapter 5

THE INFLUENCE OF THE HOLY SPIRIT IN THE WORLD

The word *influence* may bring to mind something weird or strange. But the Holy Ghost is very influential in the world today. *Influence* means a "power that causes an effect by indirect or tangible ways." It means to alter drastically or to change the course of a thing. Jesus drastically influenced this world. After His ascension, He handed the baton to the Holy Ghost.

In the Old Testament, the Holy Spirit moved upon situations, people, or events, and always changed them. He took an impossible situation and brought about remarkable change. When His mission was over, He returned to the One who sent Him.

The Holy Spirit often waited until the most critical moment before He showed up. This was divinely purposed so that no one or no thing would ever rob God of His glory. The Holy Spirit waited until He heard confessions like "It's too late," or "I can't," or "If God doesn't…" Then He stepped in and brought about a miracle.

Even though Jesus did tremendous works of power, He told His disciples that they would benefit more by His departure: *"Nevertheless I tell you the truth; It is expedient for you that I go away: for if I go not away, the Comforter will not come unto you; but if I depart, I will send him unto you"* (John 16:7).

Expedient means to be profitable, to be advantageous, to be necessary. Why would it be better for the Holy Ghost to come? Limited by an earthly body, Jesus could be in only one place at a time. Once the Holy Ghost was poured out, He could perform works of power wherever He found willing vessels.

The Holy Ghost is capable of changing any situation. Many people shun an anointed atmosphere because they know that it will challenge them to change. Preferring to stay where the power of God is *not moving*, they are never challenged, convicted, or transformed.

People do some things because they lack the presence of Jesus in their lives. If you knew that Jesus was right beside you, you would never do some of the things you do. The Holy Ghost makes you aware that He is watching your every move to deter you from evil.

The Transformer

But as many as received Him, to them gave He power to become the sons of God, even to them that believe on His name (John 1:12).

I pray that we as Christians never lose our conviction that God does change lives. We must protect this message. Our God enables us to make the radical changes necessary for fulfilling our purposes and responsibilities. Like the caterpillar that eats and sleeps its way into change, the process occurs gradually, but nonetheless powerfully. Many people who will rock this world are sleeping in the cocoon of obscurity, waiting for their change to come. The Scriptures declare, *"...it is high time to awake out of sleep: for now is our salvation nearer than when we believed"* (Rom. 13:11).

A memory of my twin sons playing on the floor when they were children tailors the continuity of this text for me. They were playing with a truck, contributing all the sounds of grinding gears and roaring engines. I didn't pay much attention as I began unwinding from the days stresses and challenges. Distractedly, I glanced down at the floor and noticed that the boys were now running an airplane down an imaginary runway. I asked, "What happened to the truck you were playing with?" They explained, "Daddy, this is a transformer!" I then inquired, "What is a transformer?" Their answer brought me into the presence of the Lord. They said, "It can be transformed from what it was before into whatever we want it to be!"

Suddenly I realized that God had made the *first* transformer! He created man from dust. He created him in such a way that, if need be, He could pull a woman out of him without ever having to reach back into the dust. Out of one creative act God transformed the man into a marriage. Then He transformed the marriage into a family, the family into a society. God never had to reach into the ground again because the power to transform was intrinsically placed into man. All types of potential were locked into our spirits before birth.

For the Christian, transformation at its optimum is the out-working of the internal. God placed certain things in us that must come out. We house the prophetic power of God. Every word of our personal prophetic destiny is inside us. He has ordained us to be!

Before I formed thee in the belly I knew thee; and before thou camest forth out of the womb I sanctified thee, and I ordained thee a prophet unto the nations (Jeremiah 1:5).

Only when we are weary from trying to unlock our own resources do we come to the Lord, receive Him, and allow Him to release in us the power to become whatever we need to be. Actually, isn't that what we want to know—our purpose? Then we can use the power to become who we really are. Life has chiseled many of us into mere fragments of who we were meant to be. To all who receive Him, Christ gives the power to slip out of who they were forced into being so they can transform into the individuals they were created to be.

Salvation as it relates to destiny is the God-given power to become what God has eternally decreed you were before. "Before what?" you ask—before the foundation of the world. What Christians so often refer to as *grace* truly is God's divine enablement to accomplish predestined purpose. When the Lord says to Paul, *"My grace is sufficient for thee..."* (2 Cor. 12:9), He is simply stating that His power is not intimidated by your circumstances.

You are empowered by God to reach and accomplish goals that transcend human limitations! It is important that every vessel God uses realize that he or she was able to accomplish what others could not only because God provided the grace to do so. Problems are not really problems to a person who has the grace to serve in a particular area.

How many times have people walked up to me and said, "I don't see how you can stand that!" If God has given us the grace to operate in a certain situation, those things do not affect us as they would someone else who does not have the grace to function in that area. Therefore, it is important that we not imitate other people. Assuming that we may be equally talented, we still may not be equally graced. Remember, God always empowers whomever He employs.

Ultimately, we must realize that the excellency of our gifts are of God and not of us. He doesn't need nearly as much of our contributions as we think He does. So it is God who works out the internal destinies of men. He gives us the power to become who we are eternally and internally.

Orchestrating Change

It would be a sad day for the unsaved if the Holy Spirit stopped convicting people and drawing them to the Savior: *"No man can come to me, except the Father which hath sent me draw him: and I will raise him up at the last day"* (John 6:44).

The Holy Ghost is very instrumental in bringing salvation. *"But when the Comforter is come, whom I will send unto you from the Father, even the Spirit of truth, which proceedeth from the Father, he shall testify of me"* (John 15:26).

Let's look at His work in the world today:

And when he is come, he will reprove the world of sin, and of right-eousness, and of judgment: Of sin, because they believe not on me; Of righteousness, because I go to my Father, and ye see me no more; Of judgment, because the prince of this world is judged (John 16:8-11).

According to this passage, the Holy Ghost has arrested you on three counts:

1. He has *reproved* your sin, which means "to convict, to expose, to convince of a wrong, to tell a fault."

2. He convinces you of righteousness or a right standing with God. His goodness, not your own, saves you.

3. He will convince you of judgment, not only of your future encounter with God, but also of ungodly influences that cause you to sin.

The Holy Ghost wants to orchestrate change in your life. Many are pregnant with gifts and callings and miracles. Many are long overdue, and He is inducing labor to bring forth delivery. Because you have messed up, many of you believe your calling has been annulled. The devil is a liar, for *"the gifts and calling of God are without repentance"* (Rom. 11:29). That is, they are *irrevocable*—He's not taking them back.

The Holy Ghost has come to convince and influence you to change. Dare to be different! Refuse to become a part of the mundane crowd going nowhere. Rise up and shake yourself. Find yourself a church that is reflecting change by the influence of the Holy Ghost.

Change—A Gift from God

Change is a gift from God. It is given to the person who finds himself too far removed from what he feels destiny has ordained for him. There is nothing wrong with being wrong—but there is something wrong with not making the necessary adjustments to get things right! Even within the Christian community, some do not believe in God's ability to change the human heart. This unbelief in God's ability to change causes people to judge others on the basis of their past. Dead issues are periodically revived in the mouths of gossips. Still, the Lord progressively regenerates the mind of His children. Don't assume that real change occurs without struggle and prayer. However, change can be achieved. Peter told a hostile audience, *"God exalted Him to His own right hand as Prince and Savior that He might give repentance and forgiveness of sins to Israel"* (Acts 5:31 NIV).

The Bible calls change *repentance*. Repentance is God's gift to a struggling heart who wants to find himself. The Lord wants to bring you to a place of safety and shelter. Without the Holy Spirit's help you can search and search and still not find repentance. The Lord will show the place of repentance only to those who hunger and thirst after righteousness. One moment with the Spirit of God can lead you into a place of renewal that, on your own, you would not find or enjoy.

I believe it was this kind of grace that made John Newton record, "It was grace that taught my heart to fear and grace my fears relieved. How precious did that grace appear the hour I first believed" (*Amazing Grace*, late 18th century hymn). When God gives you the grace to make changes that you know you couldn't do with your own strength, it becomes precious to you.

Jacob's brother, Esau, sought for the place of repentance and could not secure it:

> For ye know how that afterward, when he would have inherited the blessing, he was rejected: for he found no place of repentance, though he sought it carefully with tears (Hebrews 12:17).

To be transformed is to be changed. If you are not moving into your divine purpose, you desperately need to repent. *Repent* has a strong negative connotation for the person indoctrinated to believe that repentance is a fearful and dangerous action. It is not dangerous. Repentance is the prerequisite of revival. There cannot be revival without prayerful repentance. John the Baptist taught Israel, *"Repent ye: for the kingdom of heaven is at hand"* (Matt. 3:2). If God wants you to change, it is because He wants you to be prepared for what He desires to do next in your life. Get ready; the best is yet to come.

> For whom He did foreknow, He also did predestinate to be conformed to the image of His Son, that He might be the firstborn among many brethren (Romans 8:29).

> And be not conformed to this world: but be ye transformed by the renewing of your mind, that ye may prove what is that good, and acceptable, and perfect, will of God (Romans 12:2).

Influence in Five Areas

The Holy Ghost has influence over five major areas of our lives:

1. He sets the stage for the Word of God.

2. He separates and declares.

3. He gives new birth to buried seeds.

4. He wrestles with us to bring us to a deeper commitment.

5. He seeks a place to rest in authority.

Setting the Stage for the Word

The Holy Ghost sets the stage for the Word of God. "*And the earth was without form, and void; and darkness was upon the face of the deep. And the Spirit of God moved upon the face of the waters*" (Gen. 1:2).

Notice the condition of the earth: *Without form* means to lie in ruin, to be worthless, to be empty and in utter chaos. *Void* means to be empty, in an indistinguishable ruin. *Darkness* means more than the darkness we are familiar with. It means to bring misery and death.

When this world was in its utterly worthless, chaotic, miserable condition, the Spirit of God set the stage for a miracle. "*And the Spirit of God moved upon the face of the waters*" (Gen. 1:2).

Moved means to hover over, to bring warmth as a mother hen sits upon her nest. This warmth awakens the life inside the egg and stirs its desire to break forth. Life is present, but the shell must be broken. In the spirit realm we would call it a *breakthrough*.

The Spirit did the preparatory work. It was now up to the Word to give the command: "Let there be...." The Word worked in conjunction with the Spirit. The Holy Spirit first moved, setting the stage for the command and authority of the Word.

The words "Let there be" imply that another force or influence was trying to prevent the transformation from chaos and confusion. Satan is the only other force or influence at work in this world system. He tries to prevent the work of God from coming into its fullness.

Praise Ushers in the Move of the Spirit

But thou art holy, O thou that inhabitest the praises of Israel (Psalm 22:3).

When praise goes up, the blessing comes down. Praise becomes the prerequisite to your miracle. Praise brings Jesus into your situation.

If you're facing a dilemma, praise Him. If you're in a valley, praise Him. If you're going through a storm, praise Him. As you praise Him, Jesus—the Living Word of God—will walk right into your dilemma and say, "Let it be so."

When Philip was preaching in Samaria, revival broke out. (See Acts 8:5-8.)

And the angel of the Lord spake unto Philip, saying, Arise, and go toward the south unto the way that goeth down from Jerusalem unto Gaza, which is desert (Acts 8:26).

Then the Spirit said unto Philip, Go near, and join thyself to this chariot (Acts 8:29).

An angel led Philip to an Ethiopian eunuch. Notice how the Holy Spirit set the stage, but then the Word took center stage. They both worked together to convert this influential man (see Acts 8:30-38).

God promised the children of Israel that He would sustain them during their journey across the desert. (See Exod. 16:13-18.) He sent them manna (a type of the Word). Before the manna came, however, the ground would be covered with dew (a type of the Holy Spirit, the breathing presence of God). Once again the Holy Spirit set the stage for the Word.

Separating and Declaring

The Holy Spirit's influence will separate and declare. He separated light from darkness, declared what they would be, and placed them in order (see Gen. 1:4-5). He then separated the firmament and divided the waters. He called the firmament Heaven (see Gen. 1:6-8). He then separated the water from the dry land and declared the dry land to be earth; the waters He named seas (see Gen. 1:9-10).

The Holy Spirit will do the same thing in our lives. He will separate certain things from you, set limitations, and declare your destiny. God separated the children of Israel from Egypt. He set borders for them and went before them to drive out their enemies, but they had to go in and possess the Promised Land. God said:

> *Every place whereon the soles of your feet shall tread shall be yours: from the wilderness and Lebanon, from the river, the river Euphrates, even unto the uttermost sea shall your coast be* (Deuteronomy 11:24).

The Holy Spirit is separating you that He might declare on earth what Heaven has known from eternity.

Resurrecting Buried Seeds

The Holy Spirit wants to resurrect buried seeds in your life (see Gen. 1:11-12). The seeds were there, but they were obscured. God brought forth creatures from the waters (see Gen. 1:20). They were there, but the Word brought them forth from what had covered them. God commanded the earth to bring forth living creatures (see Gen. 1:24). They were there, but simply had to be brought forth.

God formed man from dust. But man, like anything else, is merely a form of what he can be before the Holy Spirit breathes into him vibrancy and freshness of life. Only then does the form become a living being.

God Mines for Gold

Job endured tremendous emotional pain and physical afflic-tion. His troubles were not only known to God but were allowed by God. Losing his sons and daughters and possessions left Job feeling very much alone. He looked at his situation from every possible angle, trying to find God.

Job finally concluded: *"But he knoweth the way that I take: when he hath tried me, I shall come forth as gold"* (Job 23:10). Until then, he would not curse God and die.

Every gold mine is hidden beneath the earth. Mining priceless jewels takes many hours of painstaking labor. Tons of earth must be removed to find the gold.

In the same way, a gold mine is buried beneath your flesh. Crucifying your flesh is excruciating, but it must occur to reveal the priceless jewels within you. Give God digging rights. After all, the mine belongs to Him. Allow Him to dig deep and bring out buried treasure.

The devil knows you're a gold mine waiting to be claimed and mined. Your adversary has covered your priceless jewels with your past, unconfessed sins, emotional traumas, and religious tradition. Little does the devil know that you have been buried alive. You merely need the Spirit to move, and the Word uncovers you. You are Heaven's best kept secret and hell's worst nightmare.

Wrestling for a Deeper Commitment

And the Lord said, My spirit shall not always strive with man, for that he also is flesh: yet his days shall be an hundred and twenty years (Genesis 6:3).

Strive in this verse means to wrestle with, to contend with, to compete against. The Holy Spirit wrestles with us to bring us to a deeper commitment.

If we could only see the different spirits and attitudes that we deal with in people. Have you ever wondered why you feel so spent and drained after ministry? Is it because of physical exertion? Partly. The majority of the battle comes from contending with opposing forces. This is why prayer is so important to any ministry.

We need the Holy Spirit to go before us, preparing people's hearts and minds for the Word. If the Holy Ghost truly comes upon you, He will change your life. You might not dance, you might not speak in tongues, but in some way you will be changed.

In these last days, we are not going to be dealing with novices from the kingdom of darkness. Generals and colonels from the pit of the damned will try to assault the church. As the Holy Spirit brings us to full submission, another influence opposes Him.

We Choose Who Wins

I read an article once about a man who had two dogs. Every weekend the owner let the dogs fight and placed bets on who would win. After several weekends, a man noticed the owner never lost a bet. He approached the owner, questioning him as to the secret of his success.

"It's very simple," replied the man. "It's my choice. If I want the one dog to win, I starve the other one."

This is true in the spirit realm. The Holy Spirit is there to wrestle and help us decide to feed our spirit while starving the flesh. The stronger one will win.

As the Holy Spirit wrestles with us, another influence is always present:

> *I find then a law, that, when I would do good, evil is present with me. For I delight in the law of God after the inward man: But I see another law in my members, warring against the law of my mind, and bringing me into captivity to the law of sin which is in my members* (Romans 7:21-23).

> *Now there was a day when the sons of God came to present themselves before the Lord, and Satan came also among them* (Job 1:6).

The spirit of lawlessness always tries to lead us away from where the Holy Spirit wants to take us. If we heed this second force, he will bring us into captivity. As we present ourselves to God, satan and his evil influence oppose, tempt, and accuse us. We choose who wins.

When Winning Is Losing

As the Holy Spirit strives with you to bring you into submission and obedience, you may be holding on to the very thing that He wants. As you walk away you may feel as though you've won, but you've actually lost.

Some of you are headed down rapids that will twist and turn you upside down and inside out. If you are persistent in your ways, God will stand by watching the fight that you think you won, but in all reality you lost.

Some of you have matured, and the Holy Spirit wants to take you higher. But it's a choice.

> *Therefore leaving the principles of the doctrine of Christ, let us go on unto perfection; not laying again the foundation of repentance from dead works, and of faith toward God, Of the doctrine of baptisms, and of laying on of hands, and of resurrection of the dead, and of eternal judgment. And this will we do, if God permit* (Hebrews 6:1-3).

We find the same words in Genesis chapter 1. *"Let us…."* God asks you to push away from the familiar into the supernatural. People resist change, but in order to get to where God wants us—and to arrive on time—you must push away.

God wanted to bring Israel into the Promised Land, a land full of milk and honey. Milk denotes sustenance; honey denotes sweetness of victory. But it was a choice.

Noah had a choice. God said, *"Come thou…"* (Gen. 7:1). He had to answer the call. Even after he got on board, he had a choice.

The ark had three levels. Level one, where he first got on board, felt the turbulence from the waves. On level three Noah rode on top of the waters and could look out a window that gave him access to God. The view was not available on level one.

Resting in Authority

The Holy Spirit seeks a place to rest in authority (see Gen. 8:8-12). The dove symbolizes the Holy Spirit (see Matt. 3:16-17). A dove flies up to 150 miles to find good migration. A dove makes its nest far above the earth, usually perched in a cleft of a rock. A dove fights for supremacy in the nest. It resists with fierce, decisive measures every species that tries to dwell in its home.

What can we conclude from this analogy?

- The Holy Spirit seeks to find migration in your life.

- The Holy Spirit will cause you to build your nest in a rock. David said: *"From the end of the earth will I cry unto thee, when my heart is overwhelmed: lead me to the rock that is higher than I"* (Ps. 61:2).

  We can attain a place in God that is higher than our problems, giving us a divine perspective. We must be led to this place. It is against our nature to want this rock. We must oppose our flesh and say, "When my spirit is overwhelmed, my spirit goes beyond nature and finds satisfaction only in the supernatural." We ask God to do something our flesh does not want: to lead us to the rock—Jesus—and away from earthly logic.

- The Holy Spirit will fight for you. He will go to war for you as strange birds seek to enter your nest.

- The Holy Spirit seeks rest for the sole of His foot (see Gen. 8:8-12). While the raven (our old nature) finds rest in an earth under judgment, the dove takes a different approach. He flew around and searched but found no place to rest. God wants to find a resting place for His authority:

Thus saith the Lord, The Heaven is my throne, and the earth is my footstool: where is the house that ye build unto me? and where is the place of my rest? (Isaiah 66:1)

Nor by the earth; for it is his footstool: neither by Jerusalem; for it is the city of the great King (Matthew 5:35).

The Holy Spirit flew on missions in the Old Testament as He rested upon Abraham, Isaac, and Jacob, but they were not the one. He flew upon Moses, enabling him to lead the exodus. He flew upon Samson and found periodic rest, but it was short-lived, as Samson slept in the lap of Delilah.

He flew upon David, saying, "Surely this is the Lord's anointed," but he became an adulterer and murderer. He loved him, but he was not the one. He flew upon Daniel, but he was not the one. He lighted upon Isaiah, but he was not the one. The prophet wrote about another one coming:

For unto us a child is born, unto us a son is given: and the government shall be upon his shoulder: and his name shall be called Wonderful, Counsellor, The mighty God, The everlasting Father, The Prince of Peace. Of the increase of his government and peace there shall be no end, upon the throne of David, and upon his Kingdom, to order it, and to establish it with judgment and with justice from henceforth even for ever. The zeal of the Lord of hosts will perform this (Isaiah 9:6-7).

He flew upon Jeremiah, but the weeping prophet wasn't the one. He then rested on Ezekiel and performed many mighty deeds, but Ezekiel was not the one.

Finally, He looked from the portals of glory and saw the One. There was only One found worthy in Heaven and earth for the dove to land on.

As Jesus stood in the Jordan, the dove descended from Heaven, saying, "I have found him whom my soul loveth." He landed upon Him, and His authority and anointing rested on Jesus. The Holy Ghost found a body to land on and to inhabit with authority.

Jesus died, but He said, "*Father, into thy hands I commend* [put into your trust] *my spirit*" (Luke 23:46). This same dove swept down from glory as a mighty rushing wind (see Acts 2:2). He found a body, the Church, to inhabit and to rest His authority upon.

Will You Clear the Runway!

As I flew into JFK airport one day, I noticed that our pilot was circling for a long time. He announced that fog had obscured the runway and he would continue to circle until the fog dissipated. After quite some time in the air, we finally were cleared to land.

In a spiritual sense, the runway was me; the jetliner was a type of the dove, the Holy Spirit. The Holy Spirit wants desperately to land. He desires to touch down upon the children of God, but we must clear ourselves and give Him permission to land. As the Holy Spirit circles, He sees some things that must be cleared from our lives before He lands.

Make room for the Holy Spirit. He wants to settle on your wounds, your past, your trauma, even your greatest weakness. But you are the key. Will you clear the runway? If not, He will circle for a while, but then He will seek another runway.

Give the Holy Ghost permission to land on your life. You'll never be the same.

Points to Ponder

The Holy Ghost makes you aware of God's presence.

You are empowered by God for success.

When praise goes up, blessing comes down.

Allow God to expose your buried treasure.

We choose who wins.

Make room for the Holy Spirit in your life.

Thoughts and Reflections

_____

_____

_____

_____

_____

_____

_____

_____

_____

_____

_____

_____

Chapter 6

THE CRY
OF A BARREN WOMB

Israelite women often wept bitterly as a result of their barrenness. Jewish women took to heart the covenant between God and Abraham that promised to bless and multiply the seed that would ultimately bring forth the Christ child. Barren women like Rachel cried out:

And when Rachel saw that she bare Jacob no children, Rachel envied her sister; and said unto Jacob, Give me children, or else I die (Genesis 30:1).

God wants His Bride, the Church, to bring forth fruit to His glory. How do we do that? Jesus said:

I am the vine, ye are the branches: He that abideth in me [remains in constant fellowship]*, and I in him, the same bringeth forth much fruit: for without me ye can do nothing* (John 15:5).

As we bear fruit, God will purge us that we might bring forth more fruit:

Every branch in me that beareth not fruit he taketh away: and every branch that beareth fruit, he purgeth it, that it may bring forth more fruit (John 15:2).

As we continue to walk in obedience, we produce much fruit that also releases our anointing. Why should we bear fruit?

Herein is my Father glorified, that ye bear much fruit; so shall ye be my disciples (John 15:8).

But we also benefit.

These things have I spoken unto you, that my joy might remain in you, and that your joy might be full (John 15:11).

We live in a despondent, depraved, and defeated society. The very thing that this world needs should be hanging on the limbs of the Church. They need love, joy, peace, the fruit of the Spirit. As the Holy Ghost saturates and fills our lives, we produce fruit. This is God's way of meeting the needs of lost humanity.

The fruit of the righteous is a tree of life; and he that winneth souls is wise (Proverbs 11:30).

Jesus told a parable about a man who found no fruit on his fig tree. Grieved at its lack of productivity, the owner wanted to cut it down. But the vinedresser asked to cultivate it one more year. If it didn't produce fruit, it would be cut down (see Luke 13:6-9).

Fruit-bearing is a serious thing with Jesus. The cry of the Church should be, "Give us children, lest we die!"

Never Satisfied

Solomon mentions four things that are never satisfied:

The horseleach hath two daughters, crying, Give, give. There are three things that are never satisfied, yea, four things say not, It is enough: The grave; and the barren womb; the earth that is not filled with water; and the fire that saith not, It is enough (Proverbs 30:15-16).

Several married couples in Scripture had intimate relations and yet lacked children: Abraham and Sarah, Isaac and Rebekah, Jacob and Rachel. These wives cried out because of a barren womb.

The same thing happens today when we merely go to church but lack intimacy with the Holy Ghost. The womb of our soul becomes barren. We need to cry out and not be satisfied until we become impregnated with the fruit of the Holy Spirit.

Do You Want Children?

Many are afraid to fall in love with the Holy Ghost because they know that commitment brings intimacy, and intimacy brings conception, and conception brings labor, and labor produces a baby. As in the natural realm, it takes an intimate relationship to conceive.

Many Christians have spiritual orgasms but never conceive a child. Many do not want children because they do not want commitment and responsibility. They do not want to endure nine months of carrying the child. Many have been impregnated by the Holy Ghost but have chosen to abort the baby. Other Christians who cannot carry their baby to term have miscarried.

The womb was designed as a receptacle for the seed of man and a place for a conceived child to develop. God gave Eve the responsibility, and the blessing, of bringing forth children (see Gen. 3:16). The Bible says Adam knew his wife (see Gen. 4:1,25). This intimate relationship gave them a son. You can trace the lineage of Christ back to the fruit of this first intimate relationship.

Mary was a virgin when the angel announced she would have a baby. She asked, *"How shall this be, seeing I know not a man?"* (Luke 1:34). This child was conceived by the anointing power of the Holy Ghost.

The angel told her:

The Holy Ghost shall come upon thee, and the power of the Highest shall overshadow thee: therefore also that holy thing which shall be born of thee shall be called the Son of God (Luke 1:35).

Three things were to happen:

1. Conception—*"Thou shalt conceive"* (Luke 1:31).

2. Intimacy—"*The Holy Ghost shall come upon thee.*"

3. Implanting of the Seed—"*The power of the Highest shall overshadow thee.*"

It was totally the work of the Holy Ghost, but He had to have a womb in which to do His work.

Who Are You Inwardly?

Man is made in God's image and likeness. We are also a triune being—body, soul, and spirit. God has saved our spirits. Our bodies are not saved. The body does not want to be holy or bring forth good fruit. Your body will never wake you up at 3 A.M. and tell you to pray. The body will never encourage you to live right. The body will never restrain you from gossiping. The body is flesh and will always be flesh.

David prayed, "*Search me, O God, and know my heart: try me, and know my thoughts*" (Ps. 139:23). What does God use to search us?

The spirit of man is the candle of the Lord, searching all the inward parts of the belly (Proverbs 20:27).

This verse shows us three truths:

1. Man is not only body and soul, but also spirit.

2. The spirit of man is the candle of the Lord.

3. The Lord uses this spirit to search the innermost being of humans.

Underneath your shout, your dance, your speaking in tongues, who are you really? This has always been the problem with man-made holiness. Trying to change a person outwardly only leaves him or her frustrated, confused, and feeling like a failure.

God does just the opposite. He changes you from the inside out. Out of the abundance of the heart the mouth speaks. Changing from the outside in has no lasting effect. It always leaves the womb barren, crying, "It's not enough!" Changing from the outside in is like painting a building without removing the trash that clutters the inside.

There is a difference between repainting and repenting. Repainting changes the outside, *repenting* changes the inside.

Renewed by the Transforming of our Minds

The Bible teaches that we are to be renewed by the transforming of our minds (see Rom. 12:2; Eph. 4:23). Only the Holy Spirit knows how to renew the mind. The struggle we have inside us is with our self-perception. Generally, our perception of ourselves is affected by those around us. Our early opinion of ourselves is deeply affected by the opinions of the authoritative figures in our formative years. If our parents tend to neglect or ignore us, it tears at our self-worth. Eventually, though, we mature to the degree where we can walk in the light of our own self-image, without it being diluted by the contributions of others.

When we experience the new birth, we again go back to the formative years of being deeply impressionable. It's important to be discerning in who we allow to influence us in the early years. Whenever we become intimate with someone, the first thing we should want to know is, "Who do you say that I am?" Our basic need is to be understood by the inner circle of people with whom we walk. However, we must be ready to abort negative, destructive information that doesn't bring us into an accelerated awareness of inner realities and strengths.

Jesus was able to ask Peter, *"Who do you say that I am?"* because He already knew the answer! (See Matthew 16:15.) To ask someone to define you without first knowing the answer within yourself is dangerous. When we ask that kind of question, without an inner awareness, we open the door for manipulation. In short, Jesus knew who He was.

The Lord wants to help you realize who you are and what you are graced to do. When you understand that He is the only One who really knows you, then you pursue Him with fierceness and determination. Pursue Him! Listen to what Paul shares at the meeting on Mars Hill.

And hath made of one blood all nations of men for to dwell on all the face of the earth, and hath determined the times before appointed, and the bounds of their habitation; that they should seek the Lord, if haply they might feel after Him, and find Him, though He be not far from every one of us: for in Him we live, and move, and have our being; as certain also of your own poets have said, For we are also His offspring (Acts 17:26-28).

The basic message of this passage is that God has set the bounds on our habitations. He knows who we are and how we are to attain. This knowledge, locked up in the counsel of God's omniscience, is the basis of our pursuit, and it is the release of that knowledge that brings immediate transformation. He knows the hope or the goal of our calling. He is not far removed from us; He reveals Himself to people who seek Him. The finders are the seekers. The door is opened only to the knockers and the gifts are given to the askers! (See Luke 11:9.) Initiation is our responsibility. Whosoever hungers and thirsts shall be filled. Remember, in every crisis He is never far from the seeker!

Transforming truths are brought forth through the birth canal of our diligence in seeking His face. It is while you are in His presence that He utters omniscient insights into your individual purpose and course. Jesus told a woman who had been wrestling with a crippling condition for 18 years that she was not really bound—that in fact she was loosed! Immediately, she was transformed by the renewing of her mind. (See Luke 13:11-13.) It is no wonder David said, *"In Thy presence is fullness of joy"* (Ps. 16:11b). The answer is in the presence—the presence of God, not man! There is a renewing word that will change your mind about your circumstance. Just when the enemy thinks he has you, transform before his very eyes!

Our Spirits Are Joined

The Spirit itself beareth witness with our spirit, that we are the children of God (Romans 8:16).

This Scripture deals with two spirits—the spirit of man and the Holy Spirit. Joined together at salvation, the Holy Spirit testifies to our spirit that we are saved.

One of the greatest blessings is that His work is invisible. He can testify in your spirit when all hell is breaking loose, and no one would know it but you.

He speaks to the very areas that you have tried to change without success. You may be tearful over these areas. You may have buried areas of your life over the years, trying to dispose of them. Something just won't let you throw them away.

Have you ever wanted something and knew it was God's will, but you just couldn't seem to get a breakthrough? As you see someone with the very thing you want, it causes a kicking inside you. This lets you know that your baby is still there. You haven't aborted or miscarried. As you walk the floor at night, the Holy Spirit's anointing lets you know it's still in you.

What happens next is simply awesome. The Holy Spirit becomes so much of a part of your life that you begin to have more than just a Sunday morning fling with Him. You begin to know the Holy Spirit and understand His purpose. You become sensitive to His feelings, which keep you from grieving the Holy Spirit. You begin to feel a burning love and appreciation for the Holy Spirit, which helps you to obey and submit to His leading. This keeps the flame of spiritual passion burning in your spirit.

As a result of your daily communion with the Holy Spirit, the barren areas in your life that have cried out for years—the spiritual womb that has never been satisfied—now becomes impregnated by the Holy Spirit.

A Deepening Relationship

A man and a woman who like each other become friends and get to know each other. As they sense a growing attachment for one another, they decide to date. As their commitment grows, they advance to a deeper level of relationship. Eventually, they become engaged. A ring signifies the bond between them. One day they stand before witnesses and enter into marriage. This causes them to share themselves in a more intimate way. Their new physical intimacy brings about conception and ultimately birth.

As the Spirit of God bears witness with our spirit, we deepen our relationship with God: *"Deep calleth unto deep at the noise of thy waterspouts: all thy waves and thy billows are gone over me"* (Ps. 42:7). God wants the Church to go beyond a surface relationship where He is just a friend.

He calls us to go steady; He then wants an engagement; ultimately, He wants an intimate relationship that joins the Holy Spirit together with our spirit. Cultivating intimacy eventually results in conception and birth. Your barren womb is no more.

Present at Birth, Manifested in Maturity

The parents each contribute a gene to their child. One gene is usually dominant. In the spirit realm, this is also true.

Certain traits are manifested in the child from each parent. The child may have physical characteristics like one of the parents: eyes, nose, hands, feet, hair color. Other traits, however, will only be known in time and with maturity.

The traits of our parents' genes are within us. Just as in the original creation, the seeds were in the ground but were locked up. The Holy Ghost worked in conjunction with the Word to bring about a release. This is why God said, "Let there be," meaning let it come forth.

God commanded Adam to know his wife and multiply. Likewise, as the Church has an intimate relationship with the Holy Ghost, we will begin to produce spiritual offspring or the fruit of the Spirit.

The angel who told Mary that she would be the mother of Jesus also listed four characteristics of the holy offspring (see Luke 1:32-33):

1. He shall be great.

2. He shall be the Son or offspring of the highest.

3. He shall be given the throne of His father David, which denotes authority.

4. He shall reign, which denotes lordship.

The Church is the Bride of Christ. We are espoused as "*a chaste virgin to Christ*" (2 Cor. 11:2). We are to supply our spiritual womb to the Holy Ghost, which allows us to release our anointing for His glory. As a result of our relationship, our barren womb, which is crying, dissatisfied, and longing for intimacy and fulfillment with Jesus, will begin to produce offspring in His likeness. Some of His traits will be obvious from the very outset, while others will need maturity and commitment to come to full fruition.

Producing Something Holy

When Jesus Christ was born of a virgin, people didn't know how to react. Shepherds heard the angels sing, "Glory to God in the highest!" They came and saw Him wrapped in swaddling clothes in a manger.

Simeon held Jesus in the temple and declared Him to be the consolation of Israel. Herod tried to kill Him. Many believed Jesus was a mere human. After hearing Him speak, however, they knew He was more than flesh.

Even though you live in a fleshly body, the Holy Ghost wants to birth in you a holy thing—an experience that goes beyond logic, human love, and mere spiritual excitement that leaves you turned on but empty. The Holy Ghost wants to impregnate you with a seed that will produce something holy in you. As long as you merely have a fling with the Holy Ghost, your womb will remain empty. If, after you have reached your climax and had your spiritual orgasm, your womb still is barren and crying out, then you have missed your purpose on earth.

It's an honor to carry something for Jesus and bring it to birth. It's an honor to look at your spiritual offspring and say, "This is born of God!" Whatever God births in you—a ministry, a book, a song, a message—you know whatever is born of God overcomes the world. This spiritual offspring has all the characteristics of its heavenly Father.

Producing the Fruit of the Spirit

You can never look at a Spirit-filled child of God and say that their fruit is the Holy Spirit. It isn't the Holy Spirit; it is merely the offspring or production of the Holy Spirit.

Fruit is something that takes time to be developed. It's just like the husband and wife who share a physical intimacy. Even though the woman conceives seed, it still takes nine months for the baby to be born. When the mother delivers the child, you merely see the end result of a nine-month progressive work.

Here's my point: The baby is not the father, but is the result of the seed of the father. The baby did not precede the father; the father preceded the baby. The baby did not produce the father; the father produced the baby.

The wife supplied the womb; the father supplied the seed; intimacy brought about conception. The child resembles its father. It has his blood, his eyes, his characteristics and features.

Likewise, the Church is the Bride of Christ. We supply the womb; the Holy Ghost supplies the seed; our relationship with God brings about conception. As we release our anointing and bring forth spiritual offspring, they should resemble the Father.

Fruit—Not Fruits—of the Spirit

But the fruit of the Spirit is love, joy, peace, longsuffering, gentleness, goodness, faith, Meekness, temperance: against such there is no law (Galatians 5:22-23).

The term *"fruits of the Spirit"* is not a scriptural term. The nine functions of the Holy Spirit mentioned in Galatians 5:22-23 do not come from nine different spirits; they are the result of one Spirit.

An orange has many sections, but it is one orange that resulted from one seed. An ear of corn has hundreds of kernels that resulted from one kernel. The ground conceived the grain and a few months later brought forth a finished product. A baby has one body but many functions that resulted from the mother conceiving the father's seed and allowing the child to develop for nine months.

The apostle Paul tells us that the nine functions, traits, or characteristics are the result of one Spirit. He calls this the *"fruit of the Spirit"* (Gal. 5:22).

No Limits!

After giving his discourse on the nine fruits of the one Spirit, the apostle Paul makes a very intriguing statement. He says, *"Against such there is no law"* (Gal. 5:23).

We have laws that define right and wrong. They also govern, regulate, or set limits on our behavior. If these limits are exceeded, you have broken the law. For example, you can drive only 70 mph on interstates in West Virginia. If this is exceeded, you have broken the law.

With this thought in mind, Paul tells us to put the pedal to the metal in regard to the fruit of the Spirit. There is no law to govern how much of these Father-like traits you can have as a child of God. Unlimited love, joy, and peace are available to you.

You Hold the Key

Do you know that no one, not even the devil, can keep you from acting like your Father in Heaven? We need to be keenly aware of the feelings of the Holy Spirit. While there are no limits on how much you look and act like your Father, we can hinder the Holy Spirit in five ways:

1. We can fail to spend intimate times alone with the Holy Spirit, resulting in our never really knowing Him. It would be like being married to a total stranger. Although you may cohabit the same house, no communication or sharing occurs.

2. We can grieve the Holy Spirit (see Eph. 4:30), which means to insult, to hurt the feeling of, or to make one sad.

3. We can quench the Holy Spirit (see I Thess. 5:19), which means to extinguish, like putting out a fire.

4. We can lie to the Holy Ghost (see Acts 5:3). The Bible says that satan filled their hearts (see Acts 5:3). The word *filled* means to cram full.

5. We can tempt the Spirit (see Acts 5:9).

We should avoid these at all costs. God forbid that we would have at our disposal the awesome power of the Holy Ghost and not seize Him. He wants to bring us into an intimate relationship with Jesus Christ that will cause us to become impregnated with destiny.

The Holy Ghost wants us to know God as Adam knew (to have closeness or intimacy with) Eve (see Gen. 4:1,25). Then we will produce the promised seed and begin to bear the fruit of the Spirit. Only when Adam knew Eve intimately did he produce offspring.

Thermometer or Thermostat?

The Holy Ghost functions like a thermostat and a thermometer. The thermometer reflects its surrounding temperature, and the thermostat controls the inside heating system that gives the thermometer its reading.

In the same way, the Holy Ghost works inside you. Your outward actions (what you say and do) reflect your temperature to those around you. Let's look at the outward manifestation of a Spirit-filled life:

> But the fruit of the Spirit is love, joy, peace, longsuffering, gentleness, goodness, faith, meekness, temperance: against such there is no law (Galatians 5:22-23).

This passage describes three sets of triplets. We will break these down and give each set a categorical name:

1. Atmosphere.

2. Attitude.

3. Attribute.

The atmosphere is your surroundings. You may find yourself in a very hostile atmosphere where the fruit and works of the flesh are being manifested. As you yield to the Holy Spirit, however, He will throw a wet blanket on the unkind thing that you wanted to say. The Holy Spirit will build a fire of His own that will bring warmth to a cold atmosphere, hope to a despairing atmosphere, joy to a saddening atmosphere, and love to a bitter, revengeful atmosphere. This is why the first three triplets—love, joy, and peace—are atmosphere-changing fruit.

The second three triplets—longsuffering, gentleness, goodness—are attitude-changing fruit. Even though we are saved and filled with the Holy Ghost, each of us has the potential to have an attitude. God sometimes lets us go through difficult situations to let us see what's really inside us. When we see our own helplessness, weaknesses, and despair, it causes us to cry out, "God, I need You!"

You may have been good to someone who later used you. You may have gone the extra mile for someone who betrayed you. You may have dealt with someone in gentleness who turned on you and abused you.

God works even in these hardships. As you cry out, God will take your inability to do what you know is right and make it a platform for His opportunity. You can bear longsuffering, gentleness, and goodness.

An attribute is simply a personality or character trait. If left to our own devices, we would make the same conclusion as the apostle Paul. *"Wretched man that I am!"* (Rom. 7:24). We may know what is right and want to do it, but we don't know how (see Rom. 7:15-25).

God does His most excellent work when the odds are against Him. He waits until the boat is full of water before He walks on top of your storm. He waits until the furnace of your trial is seven times hotter than normal to show Himself as the fourth man. He waits until Lazarus is decomposing to resurrect him. He waits until three doctors have agreed that you have an inoperable tumor before He steps in.

You have a strength that defies human logic. You have an ability to stand that you cannot attribute to anyone but God. You have a peace that even the apostle Paul couldn't understand, so he called it the *"peace of God, which passeth all understanding"* (Phil. 4:7). You have a joy that the apostle Peter could not describe, so he called it *"joy unspeakable and full of glory"* (1 Pet. 1:8).

We call this third triplet—faith, meekness, and self-control— attribute fruit because these qualities cannot be attributed to you but only to the Holy Ghost.

Within you lies the ability to become whatever you choose to be. Remember that you have a choice, and the choice does not come without a price.

Life from Death

Truth can be seen in the physical and spiritual realms. Jesus illustrated a dynamic spiritual truth with a common example:

Verily, verily, I say unto you, except a corn of wheat fall into the ground and die, it abideth alone: but if it die, it bringeth forth much fruit (John 12:24).

After a seed is dropped into the ground, its shell must die, decompose, or pass away. This outer casing has only one purpose: to house the heart of the grain, which produces new life.

This outer casing is like our flesh, which houses our soul and spirit. As we *"crucify the flesh"* (Gal. 5:24) and *"seek those things which are above"* (Col. 3:1), the life of the Spirit comes to full fruition in us.

Then we can say confidently:

I am crucified with Christ: nevertheless I live; yet not I, but Christ liveth in me: and the life which I now live in the flesh I live by the faith of the Son of God, who loved me, and gave himself for me (Galatians 2:20).

You Must Wait Patiently

When a seed is dropped into the ground and covered, it lies dormant for a season. No one can see it; no one can tell that anything is happening. But during this time the process of germination takes place. The casing is dying, the heart of grain is sprouting.

In the spiritual realm it is no different. The apostle Paul tells the Galatians, *"Mortify therefore your members which are upon the earth; for-*

nication, uncleanness, inordinate affection, evil concupiscence, and covetousness, which is idolatry" (Col. 3:5). *Mortify* is a term related to mortuary, a place where we find nothing but dead and dysfunctional bodies.

What is Paul saying? Stop your Adamic nature from being the dominant force in your life. Allow the Holy Ghost to work in you, putting to death the flesh so that new life may sprout from you.

The same principle is found in Numbers 17:1-8, where God took something seemingly dead (Aaron's rod) and caused it to bud. You may long to function and produce. If you feel barren, you know how the Jewish wives wept because of their barren wombs.

It is time for the Church, which is the Bride of Christ, to weep because of our barrenness. Within every one of you is a spirit that cries out as Jacob, "I know I am Jacob now, but within me is the desire to become Israel!"

Whose Baby Are You Carrying?

Let me close this chapter with a question: Whose baby are you carrying? In the middle of the night you feel it kicking. Some of you are long overdue, but you just felt destiny kicking to let you know satan has not aborted your baby.

Old farmers say that finding a spot of blood in the egg tells you that the rooster had been with the hen. Within your spirit is a womb that is with child of the Holy Ghost. Mary supplied the womb; the Holy Ghost supplied the seed; and the seed supplied the blood.

Every child can be traced back to its father by its DNA. Your blood type is 100 percent a result of the seed of your father. It is just normal that you begin to take on some of the character traits of your father. You may have his eyes, his hair, his nose. Someone may say you act just like your dad.

May that be said of us after we realize that we are carrying the baby of the Holy Ghost. May we cry out against mediocrity, compromise, and a spirit of indifference that only lead to a barren, unsatisfied womb. May we cry out for more revelation of His will for our lives.

Points to Ponder

Fill the womb of your spirit with the Holy Spirit.

He already knows the answer.

Keep the flame of spiritual passion burning.

Deepen your relationship with God through intimacy.

Produce something holy through the Holy Ghost.

Against such there is no law.

What is your thermometer reading?

Love, joy, peace. . .

*God **will** step in.*

Put the flesh to death.

Thoughts and Reflections

_____

_____

_____

_____

_____

_____

_____

_____

_____

_____

_____

_____

Chapter 7

REVIVING WHAT REMAINS

T he word *revelation* means to uncover a thing, to reveal, to fully disclose a matter. Revelation is an act of God that is just as real as God Himself. It is a divine blessing for an all wise, all-knowing God to uncover a matter, to reveal His will, and to manifest His plans for your life.

Revelation from God comes in three segments: past, present, and future. First, God sometimes reveals things in our past for instruction or edification. Jesus told the apostle John on the isle of Patmos, *"Write the things which thou hast seen [past], and the things which are [present]"* (Rev. 1:19). Sometimes God reaches into your storm or dilemma and tells you everything will be all right. *"Write...the things which shall be hereafter [future]"* (Rev. 1:19).

Come Up Higher

The apostle John recorded these words:

After this I looked, and, behold, a door was opened in heaven: and the first voice which I heard was as it were of a trumpet talking with me;

which said, Come up hither, and I will shew thee things which must be hereafter (Revelation 4:1).

The primary context of this verse and its primary doctrinal interpretation is thought to be the rapture of the Church. But every primary interpretation has a secondary application. God ushered the apostle Paul up to the third Heaven to receive tremendous revelation (see 2 Cor. 12:1-5).

Revelation Comes From the Spirit

Jesus declared the same thing to all seven churches in Revelation in chapters 2 and 3: *"He that hath an ear, let him hear what the Spirit saith unto the churches"* (Rev. 3:6).

First Corinthians 2:9-14 gives us some more insight into this verse. What the Spirit reveals is totally awesome. The scope of God's blessing covers what eye has not seen and what ear has not heard. It gets even more mind-blowing than that! The storehouse of God's will for our lives includes blessings that we have never even thought about—things that surpass even our wildest imaginations; things that have never even entered our hearts. That's awesome!

But God hath revealed them unto us by his Spirit: for the Spirit searcheth all things, yea, the deep things of God (1 Corinthians 2:10).

The apostle Paul calls them "the deep things of God." Many of us never get past the first oracles or the starting place with God which limits our ability to release our anointing.

The storehouse of Heaven is full. You will never exhaust its inventory of glory. If we aren't walking in such a way to access it, however, these glorious realities will never occur in our lives.

Therefore leaving the principles of the doctrine of Christ, let us go on unto perfection (Hebrews 6:1a).

This Scripture signifies that we must move away from where we first started with God.

As mentioned previously, Noah's ark was constructed with a first, second, and third floor. But the window, which gave Noah access to Heaven, was placed on the third floor. If Noah stayed on the first or second floor, he could not see out the window. We must get in a position to see.

Many Christians never access the windows of Heaven because they are still living in the outer court and have never broken through to the third dimension, the holy of holies. Many live in defeat and carnality because they have remained on the same level where they first boarded the ark of salvation.

Once there was a little boy who kept falling out of bed. His mother securely tucked him in, only to hear the thump on the floor as he fell out once again. After the third time she decided to stay at the door and see why he was falling out. She noticed the boy slept close to the edge where he first climbed in. One wrong turn caused him to fall out.

Many fall out of fellowship with God because they never move up to the third floor. This is why they feel the turbulence of the waves in every storm. They have stayed too close to where they first got in.

Don't Digress!

The seven churches discussed in Revelation represent seven ages of time beginning at approximately A.D. 96 and running to the present. More importantly, however, these seven churches represent seven stages of the church age.

In Revelation 2:1, Jesus walked in the midst of the church at Ephesus. In Revelation 3:20, He stands on the outside knocking for an entrance. This shows the digression of the church. Each one of these churches depicts our life as a child of God at one time or another.

1. We have left our first love (see Rev. 2:4).

2. We have been crushed as the church of Smyrna, a city noted for its perfume or myrrh (see Rev. 2:8).

3. We have had the spirit of Pergamos in us, which has caused others to stumble (see Rev. 2:14).

4. We have things in us that were strong but now have begun to die, as is the case with the church of Sardis (see Rev. 3:2).

This revelation came as a result of the seven spirits of God and seven stars. The seven spirits denote perfection or completion.

It is not seven different spirits, but shows the fullness of one Spirit (see Isa. 11:2). The seven stars denote the ministers. The word they preached, in conjunction with the Spirit, brought about this revelation to the churches (see Rev. 1:20).

Let's look at the message:

- God says to the churches, "I know." These are humbling—even frightening—words. Just think of all there is to know about you. God says, "I know."

- God says, "I know thy works." God looks beyond surface appearance and says, "I know what others do not know because I know the heart."

- God says, "I know your name." God knows our name or reputation. God says, "Yes, I have heard the gossip. I have heard what kind of reputation you have." Did you know that God knows your name and still loves you? He can know your reputation and still use you. He can know who you really are behind that worship, behind that song, behind that dance, behind your tongues, behind your preaching.

- God says, "I know the truth. I know your name." God knows that your name is Jacob but still asks, "What is thy name?" Anytime an all-wise, all-knowing God asks a question, it isn't for His benefit. You need to confess, "My name is Jacob." Even though He knows our name, He wants us to confess it because He is going to change our name and speak a glorious destiny over us.

My sheep hear my voice, and I know them, and they follow me (John 10:27).

Jesus knows His sheep by name, and He cares for and loves each one of them.

And unto the angel of the church in Sardis write; These things saith he that hath the seven Spirits of God, and the seven stars; I know thy works, that thou hast a name that thou livest, and art dead. Be watchful, and strengthen the things which remain, that are ready to die: for I have not found thy works perfect before God (Revelation 3:1-2).

- God sees beyond the name to the reality. Death means a separation, to cut off. It's like turning a light switch to the off position, which breaks the circuit and cuts off the power. God says, "I know that you are separated from life. Your name may say differently, but I know."

- God also reveals a blessing. Something remained to work with. Jesus said this in Revelation 3:2:

  "Be watchful." The word *watchful* means to awaken or arouse something that is at the point of dying. It isn't dead yet. If the Holy Spirit said these things which remained were ready to die, there was still a little life left. Maybe you have felt that your ministry is dead. If you feel any kick at all, you need to be aroused and to awaken because the movement tells you it's still alive.

"Strengthen the things that remain." The word *strengthen* means to solidify, to establish, to set upright again; to take something that has been weakened and build it back up. Within you are gifts, callings, and talents that have been weakened, pressed down, or held back. Your vision, dream, or desire may have been crushed. You may not have had any control over the circumstances. Perhaps your disobedience grieved the Holy Spirit. But arise, my friend! Whatever the devil did to you, he didn't complete the job. He left some strength in you.

Apostle Paul said, *"Most gladly therefore will I rather glory in my infirmities, that the power of Christ may rest upon me"* (2 Cor. 12:9). When his strength had given out and his resources were exhausted, he had no other place to turn. He could rely on no other strength but the strength that God gave him.

Your own strength is not enough, but if you will take what's left of it and give it to God, Who is more than enough, you will find Him to be sufficient.

Nehemiah looked at the ruined walls of Jerusalem and wept. He took the little bit that the devil had left and rebuilt the wall. Some of you are weeping over what the enemy has stolen from you. As you weep your way into depression and anxiety, the enemy causes you to lose focus on what is left.

O Lord, how many are my foes! How many rise up against me! Many are saying of me, "God will not deliver him." Selah. But You are a shield around me, O Lord; You bestow glory on me and lift up my head. To

the Lord I cry aloud, and He answers me from His holy hill. Selah
(Psalm 3:1-4 NIV).

I laid me down and slept; I awaked; for the Lord sustained me (Psalm
3:5).

David declares that it is the Lord who sustains you in the per-
ilous times of inner struggle and warfare. It is the precious peace
of God that eases your tension when you are trying to make deci-
sions in the face of criticism and cynicism. When you realize that
some people do not want you to be successful, the pressure
mounts, drastically. Many have said, "God will not deliver him."
However, many saying it still doesn't make it true. I believe that the
safest place in the whole world is in the will of God. If you align
your plan with His purpose, success is imminent! However, if I
have not been as successful as I would like to be, then seeking the
purpose of God inevitably enriches my resources and makes the
impossible attainable. If the storm comes and I know I am in the
will of God, then little else matters.

I remember when my wife and I were raising our first two children. Times were tough and money was scarce. I am not the kind
of husband who doesn't care about the provisions of the Lord in
his house. So many were the nights when I languished over the
needs in our home. Tossing and turning, praying and worrying—
I wasn't sure we were going to survive the struggle.

During these times, satan showed me images of my family
wrapped up in dirty quilts, nestled under a bridge with a burning
55-gallon drum as the only source of heat. He is such a sadist. I

was nearly frazzled with stress trying to raise the standard of our living.

I prayed, or, more accurately, I complained to God. I explained to Him how I was living closer to Him than I had ever lived and yet we were suffering with utility bills and lack of groceries. I wondered, "Where are You, Lord?" I was a preacher and a pastor. All the other men of God seemed to have abundance, yet I was in need. My car looked so bad that when we had guests in the church, one of my deacons volunteered to hide it for me behind the building. I watched my wife boil water to give us hot baths. The gas was off and sometimes the lights. I was preaching, singing, and shouting, but inside the tremors of an earthquake of frustration began to swell.

Then the car broke down. It didn't have too far to go because it was already at death's door. The only way to fix that car was to commit the body to the ground and give the engine to the Lord. At the time, though, I needed to get uptown to ask the electric company not to cut off the only utility I had left. I caught the bus to town, and walked into the office prepared to beg, but not prepared to pay. I pleaded with the young lady; I promised her money. Nothing seemed to move her, and she cut it off anyway. I was crushed. I had been laid off from my job, and my church was so poor it couldn't even pay attention. I was in trouble. I walked out of the utility office and burst into tears. I don't mean the quiet leaking of the tear ducts, either. I mean a deluge of sobbing, heaving, quaking, and wailing. I looked like an insane person walking down the street. I was at the end of my rope.

To this melodramatic outburst God said absolutely nothing. He waited until I had gained some slight level of composure and then spoke. I will never forget the sweet sound of His voice beneath the broken breathing of my fearful frustration. He said, in the rich tones of clarinet-type voice, "I will not suffer thy foot to be moved!" That was all He said, but it was how He said it that caused worship to flush the pain out of my heart. It was as if He were saying, "Who do you think that I am? I will not suffer thy foot to be moved. Don't you understand that I love you?"

I shall never forget as long as I live the holy hush and the peace of His promise that came into my spirit. Suddenly the light, the gas, and the money didn't matter. What mattered was that I knew I was not alone. He sat down beside me and we rode home smiling in each other's face—the Lord and me.

Arise

Arise, my friend, and seize what is left. So what if your joy isn't what it used to be? Use what is left. So what if your desire is dampened? Take hold of what is left. So what if your power is almost gone? Seize what is left, and be what God said you could be. Don't let circumstances abort your dream. Release your anointing.

If a person is ready to die, we don't necessarily make funeral arrangements. We care for and nourish the little life that remains. Sometimes we have to put them in the ICU, but we don't give up. Sometimes we do extensive surgery, but we don't give up. Sometimes we put them on life support. A machine may assist them in breathing, but we don't give up until they are stable enough to breathe on their own.

Satan would love to see you say the last rites over your ministry or your dreams. If you feel near death spiritually, don't major on the fact that you are dying; major on the fact that you are half alive.

In the parable of the Good Samaritan, Jesus said the thieves left the man *"half dead"* (Luke 10:30). His enemies made a big mistake. They left the man with just enough life to revive. He came back to life.

Some of you may have been diagnosed with a terminal illness. Place your case in the hands of the Great Physician. Refuse to accept the verdict. Get a second opinion.

It's Time to Take Inventory

Your miracle is not in what you lost. Your miracle is in what is left. God is not discouraged by your lack. He encourages you to rise and seize what is left.

God knows, which tells me He is not surprised. These two words may seem insignificant, but they are crucial for us to understand. You don't have to pretend. God knows everything isn't all right. God knows you aren't on top of the situation. God knows you are a 911 case. God knows you are in critical condition. In spite of your dilemma, He says, "It's not over until I say it's over."

In the midst of your trial, dilemma, or storm, do you still find a desire to overcome? Do you refuse to take no for an answer? He can take everything you have lost—your time, joy, and integrity—and bring you right up to date as though it never happened.

The miracle of His strength is that, unlike most people who are that strong about their inner worth, Christ Jesus did not wrestle with arrogance. He knew who He was, yet He *"made Himself of no reputation*" (Phil. 2:7a). When you have healthy thoughts about your own identity, it frees you from the need to impress other people. Their opinion ceases to be the shrine where you worship!

Most of us come to the Lord damaged. We're dead spiritually, damaged emotionally, and decaying physically. When He saved you, He quickened, or made alive, your dead spirit. He also promised you a new body. Then He began the massive renovation necessary to repair your damaged thoughts about life, about others, and about yourself—here come all types of nails, saws, levels, bricks, and blocks.

While we dress and smell nice outwardly, people do not hear the constant hammering and sawing going on inwardly, as the Lord works within us to present us as a newly constructed masterpiece fit for the Master's use.

The mind is continually being reconstructed by the Holy Spirit. He wants to perpetuate a new mentality within you that enables you to soar above your past. He impregnates us with hope and fills us with destiny as we release our anointing.

Give What Remains to God

Samson had lost his integrity, his hair, his strength, his looks, and his eyes. Yet, dying in the enemy's camp, he took what was left and made it available to God. God gave Samson a miracle larger than all the miracles of his entire life.

The disciples had only five barley loaves and two fish, but Jesus asked them to give it to Him. Make what you have available to God, and He will give you a miracle with what is left.

When David faced Goliath, he took off Saul's armor. The shepherd boy had only five stones. He stripped himself of everything else. But David said, *"I come to thee in the name of the Lord of hosts"* (I Sam. 17:45). He made available to God what he had left.

When the apostle Paul had gone through his storm, the ship was torn to pieces. All he had left was a board, but the board got him safely to the shores of deliverance.

The apostle John didn't have much left. All he had was a testimony, but he made it available to Him who took him higher and gave him a great revelation.

> *After this I looked, and, behold, a door was opened in heaven: and the first voice which I heard was as it were of a trumpet talking with me; which said, Come up hither, and I will shew thee things which must be hereafter* (Revelation 4:1).

The apostle refused to die until he had finished his book.

Some of you have a story to tell, a testimony to give, a book to write. Refuse to die until you have fulfilled your dream. Keep walking with God, for you *"shall not die, but live, and declare the works of the Lord"* (Ps. 118:17).

The harvest field that God wants to plant is in your head. Amid all your troubles, hold onto your field of dreams. If you can water your own field when people are trying to command a drought in your life, God will mightily sustain you. Now I know why my grandmother smiled quietly and looked distantly. She had learned the art of being her own company. She had learned how to irrigate her own mind and entertain her own hours. She was simply self-reliant, not independent (we all need other people). She had learned how to rely on her own thoughts, how to motivate her own smiles, and how to find a place of confidence and serenity within herself as she privately communed with God.

There is still much to be accomplished in the person who has maintained thoughts of greatness in the midst of degrading dilemmas. These are the smiles that paint the faces of people who know something greater and deeper, who see beyond their circumstances. They look out of the window, but they see far down the road.

If in your thoughts you see something beyond where you are, if you see a dream, a goal, or an aspiration that others would think impossible, you may have to *hold it*. Sometimes you may have to *hide it*, and most of the time you will have to *water it* as a farmer waters his crops to sustain the life in them. But always remember that they are your fields. You must eat from the garden of your own thoughts, so don't grow anything you don't want to eat. As you ponder and daydream, receive grace for the hard places and healing for the damaged soil. Just know that whenever your children, your friends, or anyone else comes to the table of your wisdom, you can only feed them *what you have grown in your own fields*. Your wisdom is so flavorful and its texture so rich that it can't be "store bought"—it must be homegrown.

A whispering prayer lies on my lips: *I pray that this word God has given me be so powerful and personal, so intimate and applicable, that it leaves behind it a barren mind made pregnant. This seed of greatness will explode in your life and harvest in your children, feeding the generations to come and changing the winds of destiny.*

Be like Enoch. He walked with God in the darkest hour that his time had ever known. It was a time of apostasy and worldliness, but he walked with God. In fact, he walked with God until, it was written, he was not. God took him higher. (See Genesis 5:24.)

No matter what they say about you, walk with God until they have to say, "He's not what we thought." Let the Holy Spirit reveal to you that there is good stuff left over after all that has happened to you. Strengthen what remains.

Points to Ponder

God's blessing covers the unseen and the unheard.

You have access to Heaven's full storehouse.

The seven spirits denote perfection.

He knows who you really are.

Within you are gifts, callings, and talents that have been weakened, pressed down, or held back.

Don't let circumstances abort your dream.

It's not over until God says so.

Trust God to give you a miracle.

Don't grow what you don't want to eat.

Thoughts and Reflections

Chapter 8

GOD'S LAYAWAY PLAN

How can you keep going when all hell has been unleashed against you? If our generation will usher in the coming of the Lord—and I believe prophecy indicates we will—then we must be equipped to face the onslaught of the devil.

All too often we have heard the story of the Gospel, but not the results of the story. Matthew, Mark, Luke, and John tell the story about the Gospel. But if we never get past the story, we fail to enter into His fullness.

The former treatise have I made, O Theophilus, of all that Jesus began both to do and teach (Acts 1:1).

This Scripture speaks about what Jesus only began to do. Throughout the epistles we find the ongoing result that the Gospel only began to tell.

God Made a Deposit

Of all the epistles that the apostle Paul wrote, one of my favorites is Ephesians. To really appreciate this letter, you must realize that it was not written from the comforts of a plush motel. Paul penned these words, the first of his prison letters, from the confines of a Roman jail.

Despite his circumstances, Paul viewed life from an eternal perspective.

> *In whom ye also trusted, after that ye heard the word of truth, the gospel of your salvation: in whom also after that ye believed, ye were sealed with that Holy Spirit of promise, which is the earnest of our inheritance until the redemption of the purchased possession, unto the praise of his glory* (Ephesians 1:13-14).

The Greek word for earnest is *arrhabon,* meaning a "pledge, a downpayment, a security deposit." It's an amount paid in advance to secure the transaction until the full price is paid to complete the purchase.

If we see a piece of property that we want but do not have the entire price, we can put a deposit or a downpayment on it. Both parties understand that a portion of the payment is still owed. This merely declares to other interested parties that the property already has a purchaser. To confirm the desire to purchase, the potential owner has given earnest money or a security deposit.

If you've ever bought merchandise on layaway, the principle is similar. You place a downpayment on your goods with the promise to pay the full amount. At regular intervals you make a payment and take the merchandise home when it has been completely paid off.

Follow the Sequence

Ephesians 1:13-14 shows us that certain things preceded the downpayment:

1. *"In whom ye also trusted"* (vs. 13). This step leads up to the downpayment. As we trust Christ as Lord and Savior, we become His purchased possession. A secular company will not put its insignia on a product it does not own. Its logo says, "This is mine. I take responsibility for it." The name seals this possession. It is a declaration of ownership.

2. *"Ye believed"* (vs. 13). It's one thing to trust when you start out, but it is a far different thing to believe when the odds say it won't happen. You have to trust God even when you can't trace Him. Believe Him when you have no visible evidence. Believe Him when everyone else has given up on you. Believe Him when you are on the mountain, but, more than that, believe Him when the mountain is on you.

It isn't always the one who is shouting and dancing who is the most anointed. The anointing falls on those who have been through the storm and stood the test, who believed through the weeping of the night. The night eventually ends, and a new day will break forth for you.

3. *"Ye were sealed with that Holy Spirit of promise"* (vs. 13). God will watch to see if you are going to trust Him. Then He will watch to see if by naked faith—without any other visible, tangible manifestation—you

are going to believe Him. Then He will seal you, and the seal carries with it a hidden blessing, the Holy Spirit of promise.

God says, "This is Mine, and I promise it will remain Mine through hell and high water because of My seal of approval. This will stand the test. This comes with a lifetime warranty. I seal it." A seal authenticates the vessel and declares, "I own all rights to this vessel. This is good stuff. It has to be, because I put My seal of approval upon it."

4. *"Which is the earnest of our inheritance"* (vs. 14). Notice what the seal stands for in the eyes of God. He wants you enough that He paid earnest money to secure the transaction. When the devil offers you the world, God says, "Sorry, devil. I began the transaction, and I will finish it! I sealed it with a promise. The transaction will not be complete until I redeem the body. Until that day comes, I own all rights. This is mine."

For Our Good

Jesus saith unto them, Did ye never read in the scriptures, The stone which the builders rejected, the same is become the head of the corner: this is the Lord's doing, and it is marvellous in our eyes? (Matthew 21:42)

Jesus concluded that the rejections of men He experienced were the doings of the Lord! As Joseph so aptly put it, "...*Ye thought evil against me; but God meant it unto good*" (Gen. 50:20a). The Lord orchestrates what the enemy does and makes it accomplish His purpose in your life. This is the Lord's doing! How many times have "evil" things happened in your life that later you realized were necessary? If I hadn't faced trials like these, I know that I wouldn't have been ready for the blessings I now enjoy.

In the hands of God, even our most painful circumstances become marvelous in our eyes! When we see how perfectly God has constructed His plan, we can laugh in the face of failure. However, *rejection is only marvelous in the eyes of someone whose heart has wholly trusted in the Lord!* Have you wholly trusted in the Lord, or are you grieving over something that someone has done—as though you have no God to direct it and no grace to correct it?

This is an important question because it challenges the perspectives you have chosen to take for your life. The statement, "It is marvelous in our eyes," simply means that from our perspective, the worst things look good! That is what you need faith to do! Faith is not needed just to remove problems; it is also needed to endure problems that seem immovable. Rest assured that even if God didn't move it, He is able! If your able God chose to stand passively by and watch someone come whose actions left you in pain, you still must trust in His sovereign grace and immutable character. He works for your good. There is a saying, "If life hands you a lemon, just make lemonade." That's cute, but the truth is, if you walk with God, He will do the squeezing and the mixing that turns lemons into lemonade!

Put Your Seat Belt On

Normally, anytime there is a crash, there is an injury. If one person collides with another, both are damaged. In the same way, a crashing relationship affects everyone associated with it, whether it is in a corporate office, a ministry, or a family. That jarring and shaking does varying degrees of damage to everyone involved. Whether we like to admit it or not, we are affected by the actions of others to various degrees. The amount of effect, though, depends on the nature of the relationship.

What is important is the fact that we don't have to die in the crashes and collisions of life. We must learn to live life with a seat belt in place, even though it is annoying to wear. Similarly, we need spiritual and emotional seat belts as well. We don't need the kind that harness us in and make us live like a mannequin; rather, we need the kind that are invisible, but greatly appreciated in a crash.

Inner assurance is the seat belt that stops you from going through the roof when you are rejected. It is inner assurance that holds you in place. It is the assurance that God is in control and that what He has determined no one can disallow! If He said He was going to bless you, then disregard them and believe a God who cannot lie. The rubbish can be cleared and the bruises can be healed. Just be sure that when the smoke clears, you are still standing. You are too important to the purpose of God to be destroyed by a situation that is only meant to give you character and direction. No matter how painful, devastated, or disappointed you may feel, you are still here. Praise God, for He will use the cornerstone developed through rejections and failed relationships to perfect what He has prepared!

Lift your voice above the screaming sirens and alarms of those whose hearts have panicked! Lift your eyes above the billowing smoke and spiraling emotions. Pull yourself up—it could have killed you, but it didn't. Announce to yourself, "I am alive. I can laugh. I can cry, and by God's grace, I can survive!"

God Seals on Earth What Heaven Has Decreed in Eternity

God has quickened us, who were once *"dead in trespasses and sins"* (Eph. 2:1). God is eternal, and the life you have is eternal. Many believe they have life but fail to understand they have eternal life. This life is not based on your merits, but it is based on *His* merits. He redeemed or bought you back.

The prefix "re" can be found throughout Scripture. God redeemed you; He reconciled you; He restored you; He regenerated you. Many times God wants us to get to the place where we realize it is all Him and not us.

Not Without a Price

If you ever get around people who have accomplished much, they will tell you that those accomplishments didn't come without price. Generally, that cost is much more expensive than you normally want to pay.

Still, the cost of total transformation means different things to different people. When you arrive at your destination, don't be surprised that some people will assume everything you achieved came without a price. The real price of success lies within the need to persevere. The trophy is never given to someone who does not complete the task. Setbacks are just setups for God to show what He is able to do. Funerals are for people who have accepted the thought that everything is over. Don't do that; instead tell the enemy, "I am not dead yet."

Jesus seldom attended funerals. When He did, it was to arrest death and stop the ceremony. If you are planning an elaborate ceremony to celebrate your nonparticipation in the plan of God, I must warn you that God doesn't hang around funerals. Sometimes Christians become frustrated and withdraw from activity on the basis of personal struggles. They think it's all over, but God says not so! The best is yet to come. The Lord doesn't like pity parties, and those who have them are shocked to find that although He is invited, He seldom attends. Many morbid mourners will come to sit with you as you weep over your dear departed dreams. But if you want the Lord to come, you mustn't tell Him that you aren't planning to get up.

> For a just man falleth seven times, and riseth up again: but the wicked shall fall into mischief (Proverbs 24:16).

The whole theme of Christianity is one of rising again. However, you can't rise until you fall. That doesn't mean you should fall into sin. It means you should allow the resurrecting power of the Holy Ghost to operate in your life regardless of whether you have fallen into sin, discouragement, apathy, or fear. There are obstacles that can trip you as you escalate toward productivity. But it doesn't matter what tripped you; it matters that you rise up.

People who never experience these things generally are people who don't do anything. There is a certain safety in being dormant. Nothing is won, but nothing is lost. I would rather walk on the water with Jesus. I would rather nearly drown and have to be saved than play it safe and never experience the miraculous.

When the AIDS epidemic hit our country, pandemonium erupted. Terror caused many people, Christians as well as non-Christians, to react out of ignorance and intimidation. The media continually presented the sickness as it attacked many individuals in highly visible positions. In listening to the discussions on television and elsewhere, the primary concern didn't seem to be for the victim.

People were whispering, wanting to know how it was contracted. I told the church I pastor that it was absolutely absurd to concern themselves with how anybody contracted AIDS. The issue is that they have it, and what are we going to do to help. It is not as though the disease is any less vicious to someone whom we approve of or exonerate—it has the same effect. Many are the methods by which we can contract it, but there will be one cure.

In that same sense, regardless of what causes us to fall, what matters is that we get up! The enemy wants to lull us into a state of acceptance whereby we consider ourselves unable to alter the circumstances that limit us. However, the just man is successful because he continues to get up. The Holy Spirit challenges us to stand in the midst of contrary winds, and if we stumble to our knees, to grasp the hand of God's grace and arise.

We Groan Because of What We Know

The apostle Paul used a two-letter word that is packed with dynamite. He mentioned the word we 11 times in Second Corinthians 5:1-8. Each time he speaks about the part of you that has received its downpayment. The "we" is not the house (our body), because the house will one day die. Because of what "we" know, the "we" in us groans.

The "we" in us is confident, the "we" in us walks, the "we" in us is willing, the "we" in us already knows what is ours. This is why we groan; this is why we walk when it doesn't look like we are going to win.

Notice what keeps the "we" in us going: *"the earnest of the Spirit"* (vs. 5). While we live in this flesh, we are absent from the Lord. But, because of the earnest (downpayment of the Spirit), we know that one day the mortal part of us will be swallowed up by the life in us.

Even though this primarily speaks of the future resurrection, knowing this can help us conquer our flesh. When our flesh tries to depress or hinder us, saying, "You won't make it," this truth enables our flesh to be swallowed up.

The earnest of the Spirit, which becomes the promise of God's approval upon your life, will swallow up your defeat and anxiety. With this downpayment it may not look good right now, but just hold on. You have God's promise.

I can't tell you enough about what this insight will do for you. Because of the earnest of the Spirit, you can always be confident.

Confident and Relentless

Several years ago a young man walked up to me and said, "I am getting ready to pioneer a church. Do you have any advice for me?" In fact, he asked, "If you could sum up in one word what it takes to be effective in ministry, what would that word be?" I thought about it a moment, then responded, "Relentless!" You must be a person who is relentless—always abounding in the work of the Lord. If you give up easily, there is no need for you to attempt to accomplish much for God. *Relentless* is the word I use to describe people who will not take no for an answer. They try things one way, and if that doesn't work, they try it another way. But they don't give up. You who are about to break beneath the stress of intense struggles, be relentless. Do not quit!

A terrible thing happens to people who give up too easily. It is called *regret*. It is the nagging, gnawing feeling that says, "If I had tried harder, I could have succeeded." When counseling married couples, I always encourage them to be sure they have done everything within their power to build a successful marriage. It is terrible to lay down at night thinking, "I wonder what would have happened if I had tried that."

Granted, we all experience some degree of failure. That is how we learn and grow. If a baby had to learn how to walk without falling, he would never learn. A baby learns as much from falling on his bottom as he does from his first wobbly steps. The problem isn't failure; it is when we fail and question if it was our lack of commitment that allowed us to forfeit an opportunity to turn the test into a triumph! We can never be sure of the answer unless we rally our talents, muster our courage, have faith and hope, and focus our strength to achieve a goal. If we don't have hope and a passion to be relentless, then we will not succeed.

Hope Will Change Us

What did the apostle Paul say?

And not only they, but ourselves also, which have the firstfruits of the Spirit, even we ourselves groan within ourselves, waiting for the adoption, to wit, the redemption of our body (Romans 8:23).

The spirit is saved by faith, and the body is saved by hope.

Hope purifies our soul. When it doesn't look good, hope says, "It's all right." This is why we need such a strong witness in our soul. God gives us hope in the midst of our storm.

We must understand the working of the Holy Spirit in our lives. Many become discouraged when they fall short of their goals as a child of God. Others throw in the towel and say, "What's the use?"

Many of you are near a breakthrough in your life. You may have fought for years to get to where you are with God. Many of you are pregnant with destiny. You are carrying within the womb of your spirit a ministry that could change this world.

It's All in a Place

Moses was in the same place where we often find ourselves— near burnout. He had been functioning and abiding in the call of

God for his life. Yet he longed for a manifestation of God's presence. Moses prayed, *"I beseech thee, shew me thy glory"* (Exod. 33:18).

God wants to show us His glory and splendor as much as, if not more than, we want to see it. In order for us to see the glory of God, however, we must get to the place. God told Moses: *"And the Lord said, Behold, there is a place by me, and thou shalt stand upon a rock"* (Exod. 33:21).

Remember, whenever God got ready to manifest Himself in glory and splendor, He always took the person up to a mountain or an elevated domain. Then He would manifest Himself.

God promised Moses that he would see His glory, but only after Moses got to a certain place. The apostle Peter had a revelation by the Spirit regarding Christ (see Matt. 16:13-18). Jesus is the Rock, and when we hide ourselves in Him we are taken to higher heights and deeper depths.

A cleft is a small crevice or opening. When the soldier pierced the side of Jesus, a cleft opened. We are able, by the Holy Ghost, to hide in this cleft. God promised Moses:

> *I will make all my goodness pass before thee, and I will proclaim the name of the Lord before thee....And it shall come to pass, while my glory passeth by, that I will put thee in a cleft of the rock, and will cover thee with my hand while I pass by: And I will take away mine hand, and thou shalt see my back parts: but my face shall not be seen* (Exodus 33:19-23).

Moses saw only the afterglow of God's glory, but he was greatly affected.

The children of Israel saw the face of Moses, that the skin of Moses' face shone: and Moses put the veil upon his face (Exodus 34:35).

Some of you are going through a storm, a trial, or something you don't even understand. You're saying to yourself, "I've been faithful. I'm committed to my call. I've exercised my gift, but I still don't understand why this is happening to me."

Don't lose your focus. Help is on the way. What you face will be nothing more than a cleft in the rock. As you go through this problem, you will begin to understand the words of the old hymn, "Rock of Ages, Cleft for Me."

This very storm is taking you to higher ground. Let God raise you to another level through this trial. Noah let a torrential downpour and a flood take him to higher ground. His ark landed upon Mt. Ararat (see Gen. 8:1-4).

God Inhabits an Old House

Within our decaying shells, we constantly peel away, by faith, the lusts and jealousies that adorn the walls of our hearts. If the angels were to stroll through the earth with the Creator and ask, "Which house is Yours?" He would pass by all the mansions and cathedrals, all the temples and castles. Unashamedly, He would point at you and me and say, "That is Mine!" Imagine the shock and disdain of the heavenly host to think that the God whose face they fan with their wings would choose to live in such a shack and shanty! We know where our greatest conflict lies. We who blunder and stumble in our humanity, we who stagger through *our frail exis-*

tence—we continually wrestle with the knowledge that our God has put so much in so little!

Yes, it is true: Despite all our washing and painting, all our grooming and exercising, this old house is still falling apart. We train it and teach it. We buy books and tapes, and we desperately try to convince it to at least think differently. But like a squeaky hinge on a swollen door, the results of our efforts, at best, come slowly. There is no doubt that we have been saved, and *there is no doubt that the house is haunted.* The Holy Ghost Himself resides beneath this sagging roof. (Although the tenant is prestigious, the accommodations are still substandard.)

This divine occupation is not an act of a desperate guest who, having no place else to stay, chose this impoverished site as a temporary place to "ride out" the storm of some deplorable situation. No, God Himself has—of His own free will and predetermined purpose—put us in the embarrassing situation of entertaining a Guest whose lofty stature so far exceeds us that we hardly know how to serve Him!

The very best of us camouflage the very worst in us with religious colloquialisms that reduce Christianity to more of an act than an attitude. Even the most pious among us—while in the quiet booth of some confessional or kneeling in solitude at the edge of our beds—must murmur our confession before God: We have earnestly pursued a place in You that we have not attained.

Our struggle continues to feed the ravenous appetite of our holy Guest, whose divine hunger requires us to perpetually feed Him a sacrificial life. He daily consumes, and continually requires, that which we alone know God wants from us. Paul battled to bring into submission the hidden things in his life that could bring destruction. Perhaps they were putrid thoughts, or vain imaginations, or pride—but whatever they were, he declared war on them if they resisted change. He says, in essence, that as he waits for the change, he keeps his body in chains, beating back the forces of evil: *"But I keep under my body, and bring it into subjection: lest that by any means, when I have preached to others, I myself should be a castaway"* (1 Cor. 9:27).

With a testimony like this, I pay very little attention to those among us who feel obligated to impress us with the ludicrous idea that they have already attained what is meant to be a lifelong pursuit. The renewal of the old person is a daily exercise of the heart. It progressively strengthens the character day by day, not overnight!

You'll Never Be the Same

As Moses spent time on the mountain with God, he began to take on the appearance of God. When Moses came down from the mountain, he had to veil his face to be able to talk with the people. The glory of God was so evident that the people could not look upon him because of the brightness of his countenance.

The apostle Paul asked this question:

But if the ministration of death, written and engraven in stones, was glorious, so that the children of Israel could not stedfastly behold the face of Moses for the glory of his countenance; which glory was to be done away: How shall not the ministration of the spirit be rather glorious? For if the ministration of condemnation be glory, much more doth the ministration of righteousness exceed in glory (2 Corinthians 3:7-9).

The glory of the new covenant and the ministry of righteousness far exceed the ministry of death that came through the law. The apostle Paul closes that chapter with this thought:

> *But we all, with open face beholding as in a glass the glory of the Lord, are changed into the same image from glory to glory, even as by the Spirit of the Lord* (2 Corinthians 3:18).

Open God's Word and allow it to become a mirror. As the Holy Ghost illuminates your life, you will begin to reflect His glory as Moses did. Be willing to pay the price and discipline yourself, because God wants to do a work in your life, your ministry, your marriage, and your calling.

Stripped Down to the Eternal

Jesus laid aside His garments. That is what ministry is all about. It requires you to lay aside your garments. Lay aside your personal ambitions and the visions of grandeur. Gifted people tend to be some of the most egotistical, self-aggrandizing, eccentric individuals the world has ever seen. That is why "being gifted" in itself will never deliver anybody. Ministry is birthed when you are stripped down to your heart's desire, when beneath every other thread of whimsical grandeur, something in your heart says more than anything else, *I want my life to have counted for something. I want to accomplish something for God.*

Have you ever prayed the kind of prayer that pleads, "Oh God, don't let me impress anyone else but the One to whom I gave my life"?

Have we given our lives to the Lord? I am absolutely serious— I'm talking to those of us who witness and work in the Kingdom trying to bring souls to God. Have we given our lives to the God we teach about? If we have, then why are we still standing around the table arguing over who is going to sit on the left and who is going to sit on the right? *Why have we not laid aside our garments?*

The garment represents different things to different people. It is whatever camouflages our realness, whatever hinders us from really affecting our environment. Our garments are the personal agendas that we have set for ourselves (many of which God was never consulted about). Like the fig leaves sewn together in the garden, we have contrived our own coverings. The terrible tragedy of it all is that, sooner or later, whatever we have sown together will ultimately be stripped away.

The Lord often uses trials to realign us. The strong winds of adversity will attack everything in us that can be shaken. Weaned by the wind, we release every idol in His presence. Every person who finds real purpose will, sooner or later, go through some series of adversities that will cause them to let go of the temporal and cleave to the eternal. Some awaken in hospital rooms with respirators and monitors beeping in their ears. There, beneath the quiet canopy of painted ceilings and with the soft smell of disinfectant, they realize that many of the things that seemed important mean nothing at all.

Left with nothing of importance but the simplicity of a second chance, they lay there. Their certificates of deposit in the bank, their cars in the garage, and their clothes somewhere in a closet, have all lost their importance. Beneath those thin, frail hospital sheets, they discover they are really no different from "Joe

Poor" down the hallway, who is there on his Medicaid card. They are stripped beneath the sheets and, for the first time, they don't care to read the paper, check the stocks, or catch the news. At least for a while, they are *naked and not ashamed!*

You can never be really anointed until you personally experience a situation that calls you to lay aside your garments. It is from this river that the tears of worship are born. They fall lavishly down a face that has been pulled from behind its covering and laid bare before God. Who can help but worship Him, once we see Him aside from every distraction and weight?

The glamorous Prince of Peace stripped Himself. As He knelt down on the floor and began to wash the disciples' feet, He looked so lowly that it was embarrassing. Peter almost refused to allow Him to be seen in that light. To think that the One he called Master would appear in a towel! One moment He was as stately as a prince, and the next moment He knelt naked before them as just a man.

The Anointing

There is a price to pay to be anointed of God—and an even greater price to maintain your anointing. The Holy Ghost has sealed you, which is a downpayment on this great blessing that God is preparing you for.

As far as God is concerned, it's done.

Points to Ponder

Believe through the weeping unto the new day's dawn.

Trust His marvelous plan!

"I'm not dead yet!"

Grasp God's hand of grace and arise.

Do not quit!

So much in so little.

The glory of God was obviously evident.

Lay aside your garments.

Release your anointing!

Thoughts and Reflections

RELEASE
YOUR
DESTINY,
RELEASE
YOUR
ANOINTING
EXPANDED
EDITION

STUDY GUIDE

DAY 1

HUMANKIND IS BODY, SOUL, AND SPIRIT

And I pray God your whole spirit and soul and body be preserved blameless unto the coming of our Lord Jesus Christ (1 Thessalonians 5:23).

Excerpt: *Release Your Anointing Expanded Edition*, Chapter 1.

This Scripture shows the three parts of humankind: body, soul, and spirit. If we want to have a successful prayer life and reach our full potential with God, each of these parts must be understood.

All three affect our prayer life. If we were only spirit, the blessings of prayer would be unrestrained, without hindrance. But we also have to deal with our body and soul.

The words *wholly* and *preserved* are significant. *Wholly* means to completely, absolutely reach the limit or potential. *Preserved* means to guard, to watch, to keep an eye on, to keep something in its place. As we pray, we must contend with these three parts.

1. Body

This entails our flesh and its appetites. The flesh never wants to pray.

2. Soul

The soul is sandwiched between our body, which never wants to pray or do right, and our spirit, which desires God and spiritual things. The soul entails our emotions, feelings, weaknesses, and our past.

3. Spirit

Now that you are saved, your spirit has been quickened. As the Holy Ghost begins to have an intimate relationship with our spirit, we begin to produce the *"fruit of the Spirit"* (Gal. 5:22-23).

Your Thoughts

I. If you were to explain the three parts of humankind to someone who does not know biblical terms, what would you say? To your understanding, how do these three parts work together?

_____

_____

_____

_____

2. What does First Thessalonians 5:23 mean to you? What does *blameless* mean to you? Do you believe you can be "blameless"?

_____

_____

_____

3. In what way does your body participate in prayer? Why do you think it is so resistant to prayer? In what ways do you have to make the body submit to discipline?

_____

_____

4. In what way does your soul participate in prayer? How do you think your soul bridges between the body and the spirit? What part of your soul seems the most unruly or challenging to tame?

_____

_____

_____

5. In what way does your spirit participate in prayer? How does the Holy Spirit commune with a person's spirit? What are the results that you have seen from this type of communion?

_____

_____

_____

_____

_____

_____

Meditation

"Apostle Paul wrote, *'that I may know Him'* (Phil. 3:10), which implies a close relationship—one that causes us to partake in His experiences. But you can't know Christ in resurrection power until you know Him in His sufferings and death. Our old man must be crucified with Him daily as we are being changed from glory to glory."

What do you think Paul meant by wanting to "know" Christ? How well do you know Christ? How much do you participate in His sufferings and death as well as His resurrection power?

DAY 2

HELP IN PRAYER

Likewise the Spirit also helpeth our infirmities: for we know not what we should pray for as we ought: but the Spirit itself maketh intercession for us with groanings which cannot be uttered. And He that searcheth the hearts knoweth what is the mind of the Spirit, because He maketh intercession for the saints according to the will of God (Romans 8:26-27).

Excerpt: *Release Your Anointing Expanded Edition,* Chapter 1.

The Holy Ghost stands alongside us to assist, to cause one to stand, to cause one to achieve. He stands by your side to plead the covenant of God and cause you to attain what the covenant provides for you.

He does this in four ways:

1. He assists us through our *infirmities*. The word infirmities means "inability to produce results." The Holy Ghost helps us and gives us a breakthrough.

2. He assists us in that He knows. The Spirit is very knowledgeable about things that perplex us. We don't

always know what is right. He begins to tell us how to pray for certain things.

3. He assists us with intercessions. "He maketh intercession for us." Intercession means that the Holy Ghost will meet with us. He comes into our situation and speaks into our spirit as one who interviews another.

4. He assists us with Heaven's language. The Spirit pleads the will of God to us. As creation groans, it speaks a language that only God can interpret.

The Holy Ghost is one with God. He will never speak anything that is not sanctioned by the Word.

Your Thoughts

1. Have you ever experienced the Holy Ghost assisting you in some area that you felt you could not do on your own? What part does the Holy Ghost play in assisting us in prayer?

_____

_____

_____

_____

2. Have you ever experienced the Holy Ghost helping you stand when you felt you would fall down either spiritually, emotionally, mentally, or physically? How does the Holy do this kind of work for us?

    _____

    _____

3. Have you ever experienced the Holy Ghost helping you to achieve something that seemed out of reach in your own power? How does the Holy Spirit make a difference in these types of situations?

    _____

    _____

4. Look through the list of four ways God assists us. How is each of these areas important to us personally if we are to grow into Christ's likeness or bring glory to God?

    _____

    _____

    _____

5. How does the Oneness of the Holy Ghost with the Father bring credibility to what the Holy Spirit does? How does this resemble what Jesus said about what He did while on earth?

_____

_____

_____

_____

Meditation

In John 16:13, Jesus said the Holy Ghost would do four things:

1. Guide you into all truth.

2. Speak truth to you, but not speak of Himself.

3. Show you all truth concerning things to come.

4. Speak into you what He hears Heaven speaking.

We must be able to hear what He is saying. But it is equally important to know the Holy Ghost hears what to speak to us.

Think through the four things listed. Have you experienced each of these personally? Why do you think it is so important to know that the Holy Spirit does not compose His own words to us?

DAY 3

BUILD UP YOURSELF

But ye, beloved, building up yourselves on your most holy faith, praying in the Holy Ghost, keep yourselves in the love of God, looking for the mercy of our Lord Jesus Christ unto eternal life. And of some have compassion, making a difference: And others save with fear, pulling them out of the fire; hating even the garment spotted by the flesh (Jude 20-23).

Excerpt: *Release Your Anointing Expanded Edition*, Chapter I.

The word *build* is an architectural word that means "to cause a building to stand." It means "to lay a good foundation." In the natural realm, it is always important to leave yourself the ability to add on to your building in case you need to expand in the future. If you have outgrown your spiritual house, the Holy Ghost gives you the resources to add on to meet your demands.

Are there weak areas in the structure? Build them up. You do this by praying in the Holy Spirit.

God leads you through a progressive path, but the ultimate goal is to be fruitful. Like Elijah, He wants you to be able to call fire down from Heaven, to see into the Spirit, and to persevere in prayer until God intervenes in your situation. The answer to your drought may appear to be a cloud the size of a man's hand, but you know a refreshing rain is about to fall.

This is why Christians from all denominations are being filled with the Holy Ghost. Having outgrown the tradition of their past experiences, they have passed the tests and are ready for fruitfulness.

Your Thoughts

1. Think through Jude 20-23 and consider the impact of the words on your life. Do you regularly obey the admonitions contained in the verses?

_____

_____

2. How are we to build a good foundation for our spiritual house? What are the elements of a good foundation?

_____

_____

_____

3. Do you think you have outgrown your spiritual house? How can you tell? What signs are there that God wants you to have more?

———————————————————

———————————————————

———————————————————

4. How does the progressive path God gives us allow us to take steps forward without stumbling? How can we recognize this path so we continue to move forward instead of standing still without motion?

———————————————————

———————————————————

———————————————————

5. Why do we need to get rid of traditions in order to progress in God? Do you have any traditions that you need to leave behind in order to move forward to fruitfulness?

———————————————————

———————————————————

Meditation

If you feel a hunger to go on with God, the Holy Ghost is telling you that your current spiritual house is too small. He is urging you to build on your foundation. In order to do this, however, we must pray in the Holy Ghost.

Where is your spiritual house? What does it mean that it is "too small"? Take time to ask the Lord to build on your foundation. Take time to pray in the Holy Ghost.

DAY 4

MORE BENEFITS OF PRAYING IN TONGUES

What is it then? I will pray with the spirit, and I will pray with the understanding also: I will sing with the spirit, and I will sing with the understanding also (I Corinthians 14:15).

Excerpt: *Release Your Anointing Expanded Edition*, Chapter I.

Unlike giving a message in tongues in a public meeting, which edifies other people, *praying* in tongues edifies you.

Praying in tongues does at least five things for you individually:

1. Praying in tongues gives you the ability to talk to God alone, frustrating the devil. Praying in tongues enables you to bypass satan's radar system.

2. Praying in tongues edifies the person praying. As you pray in tongues, you enlarge your borders.

3. Praying in tongues helps you put on the armor of God. This armor dresses you for any occasion.

4. Praying in tongues builds up a wall of defense. The Holy Spirit stands by as your ally.

5. Praying in tongues helps you relieve anxiety. Praying in the Spirit allows you to *come apart* before you *come apart*. Like Jesus, you need a solitary place to rest awhile.

That's why we need to pray within the spirit realm, which is bigger than any problem, weakness, or dilemma we face. We also need to ask God to interpret to us the things that we have spoken through the auspice of the Holy Ghost. As He reveals them to us, we will gain understanding.

Your Thoughts

1. How does praying in tongues give you the ability to bypass satan and talk to God alone? How does it frustrate the devil?

_____

_____

_____

_____

_____

2. Define *edify* in your own words. How does praying in tongues edify you? What does it mean to "enlarge your borders"? Have you enlarged your borders?

_____

_____

_____

3. Can you name the pieces of the armor of God that are mentioned in Ephesians 6? How does praying in tongues help you dress yourself in these pieces of armor? How does this make us ready for whatever happens?

_____

_____

4. How does praying in tongues help us build up a wall of defense? What kind of defense is made on your behalf? How does the Holy Spirit become your ally?

_____

_____

_____

5. In what way does praying in tongues help to relieve
    your anxiety? How does this help you get away from
    earthly cares and distractions?

_____

_____

_____

_____

_____

_____

Meditation

"Praying in the Spirit pulls us into an experience with God.
It's not surprising that Paul wondered whether he was in the body
or out of the body. The apostle saw and heard things unlawful for
a man to speak. God in the Spirit takes us to paradise, pulling us
apart from the pressures of the world before we are pulled apart."

Have you ever felt spiritually blah, but after praying in the
Spirit, felt pulled into an experience with God? What benefits of
paradise could you use right now?

DAY 5

WE NEED THE ANOINTING

Wherefore seeing we also are compassed about with so great a cloud of witnesses, let us lay aside every weight, and the sin which doth so easily beset us, and let us run with patience the race that is set before us (Hebrews 12:1).

Excerpt: *Release Your Anointing Expanded Edition*, Chapter 1.

Sometimes we don't know what to say. Our hearts are crushed; our spirits are overwhelmed. We know that we need a touch. We know the area that needs to be touched, but we don't always know what to say.

Have you ever been so overwhelmed, so overcome that all you can do is groan? Maybe you can only say, "Jesus, help me," or "I need You, Lord." That's when we need to change our language. We need to wait on the Holy Ghost because He knows how to pray—and what to pray. The Holy Ghost will always pray in alignment with the will of God (see Rom. 8:27).

In these last days, satan and all his cohorts are waging a final onslaught against the Church. We must know God in a way in which we have never known Him before. Within you are miracles, unborn babies, ministries, and gifts. We all have callings.

Your Thoughts

1. The anointing brings power. How can you tap into that power to overcome the enemy's attacks?

_____

_____

_____

_____

_____

2. God shows Himself in the holy of holies (see Exod. 25:17-22). Have you been there? Has He revealed Himself to you as promised? If not, why do you think that is?

_____

_____

_____

3. What miracles do you think are within you? How is satan keeping you from birthing those miracles?

_____

_____

_____

4. Scripture tells us *"the gifts and callings of God are without repentance"* (Rom. 11:29). You can release your anointing when you can see the raw, undiluted presence of God. Are you actively looking for Him?

_____

_____

_____

5. Have you allowed satan to veil your mind to God's presence because of past failures or experiences? What can you do to unveil the beauty within?

_____

_____

_____

Meditation

"The anointing of the Holy Ghost doesn't always bring chills or goosebumps. It isn't always charged with emotion.… You need to get to where you can see the raw, undiluted presence of God and His anointing. Only then can you release your anointing to bring glory to His Kingdom."

Are you afraid to give total control of your life, spirit, soul, and body to the Holy Ghost? What is the worse-case scenario that you can imagine if you did give Him total control? What is the best-case scenario that you can imagine? Choose today.

DAY 6

YOU CAN RECEIVE THE HOLY GHOST

And I will pray the Father, and He shall give you another Comforter, that He may abide with you forever (John 14:16).

Excerpt: *Release Your Anointing Expanded Edition*, Chapter 2.

You have the right to receive the Holy Ghost because Jesus prayed for you to receive Him.

The Holy Ghost has been given to assist us in a variety of ways. He helps to guide us (see John 16:13). He assures us that we are children of God (see Rom. 8:16). He gives us power to witness (see Acts 1:8). He helps us to pray (see Rom. 8:26). He enables us to bear the fruit of the Spirit (see Gal. 5:22-23).

The Holy Ghost is always present. He is our backup! The Holy Ghost stands by the children of God to assist them in carrying out the same work—and even "greater works" (see John 14:12). Believers must understand the ministry of the Holy Ghost so they can carry out the will of God for their lives.

We aren't alone when we lie down at night or go through the storms of life. When we go through a valley or through a trial, the Holy Ghost is there to defend us. When we receive the fullness of the Holy Ghost, we receive an eternal friend. Jesus is praying that you have an intimate relationship with the Holy Ghost.

Your Thoughts

1. If Jesus prayed that we would receive the Holy Ghost, does this make the act of receiving Him optional or mandatory? Why do you think it is so important that we receive this part of the Trinity?

_____

_____

2. Have you seen the Holy Ghost's assistance in your life or in the life of others around you in the following areas: guidance; assurance; witnessing; prayer; bearing fruit? How can you tell if it is the Holy Spirit who is assisting the believer?

_____

_____

3. Why is the Holy Spirit so important to our ministry on earth? What does the Holy Spirit do to enable us to carry out the will of the Father?

_____

_____

4. Has the Holy Ghost's presence been made real to you in any specific way in terms of your life experiences? If so, relate an incident or events that demonstrated His presence. If not, what do you think His presence would be like?

_____

_____

5. What do you think it means to be an "eternal friend" of the Holy Ghost? What would characterize an "intimate relationship" with Him?

_____

_____

Meditation

"Many friends stay with us until we mess up or until we disagree with them. They quickly leave as if they never knew us. But the Holy Ghost, our Comforter, stays with us forever. The Holy Ghost does not come and go based on the circumstances of our lives. In the same way that Jesus helped the disciples, the Holy Ghost now helps us."

Since the Holy Ghost does not abandon us when we are in trouble or sin, what do we need to do to depend on His friendship in the midst of trials? What do you think it takes for us to become more dependent on Him than on ourselves when we mess up?

DAY 7

WHEN DO WE
RECEIVE THE HOLY GHOST?

And, behold, I send the promise of My Father upon you: but tarry ye in the city of Jerusalem, until ye be endued with power from on high (Luke 24:49).

Excerpt: *Release Your Anointing Expanded Edition*, Chapter 2.

God's Word shows that a person receives the Holy Ghost as a mark of identity, confirming that he or she really is a child of God (see John 3:5-6; Rom. 8:9,14-16; Gal. 4:6).

The apostle Paul commanded the Ephesian believers to *"be filled with the Spirit"* (Eph. 5:18). They had already been saved by the grace of God (see Eph. 2:8-9), and had been sealed by the Holy Ghost (see Eph. 1:13).

Despite these things, apostle Paul admonished them to be filled with the Holy Ghost.

In order for the Ephesians to be happy and bold, to walk in the will of God, to talk in a new way, and not be afraid of their future, they needed to be filled with the Holy Ghost.

Ephesians closes with a discussion of the battle that we face as children of God. If we are to partake of the blessings that God has predestined for us; if we are to be the workmanship of God; if we are to enjoy a happy marriage and rear children in the fear and admonition of the Lord; we will face a spiritual battle. Living a Spirit-filled life, however, abundantly equips us to carry out these tasks.

Your Thoughts

1. How do you think that receiving the Holy Ghost gives a believer a "mark" of identity? Is this mark a visible sign? How do you think this identity is perceived by others?

   _____

   _____

   _____

2. When we are saved by grace, how does the Holy Spirit woo us to the cross of Christ? How is this different than being filled with the Spirit?

   _____

   _____

   _____

3. What benefits does the believer have when filled with the Holy Spirit? Have you personally experienced any of the benefits you named?

_____

_____

_____

4. Why do you think the Holy Spirit is such a necessary part of walking in the will of God? What kind of difference do you think the Holy Spirit makes so we can fulfill God's will?

_____

_____

5. How dramatic has the Holy Spirit been in your own life in terms of your family relationships, the blessings you have received, the challenges you have faced, the battles you have won, and the fulfillment of the destiny God has worked within you?

_____

_____

Meditation

You can be saved, but not necessarily filled or baptized with the Holy Ghost. We receive the Holy Ghost as a mark of identity when we are saved, but another experience—the baptism in the Holy Ghost—awaits us. The believers in Acts 10:44-46 and Acts 19:1-7 had not been baptized in or received the infilling of the Holy Ghost. Peter and Paul found it necessary to address this.

Do you see any difference between Christians who have received salvation and those who have gone on to receive the baptism of the Holy Spirit? Is there a distinction in your life so people can tell the difference the Holy Spirit has made in you? Are you "visibly" marked?

DAY 8

WE MUST *SEEK*
WHAT WE ASK FOR

And I say unto you, Ask, and it shall be given you; seek, and ye shall find; knock, and it shall be opened unto you. For every one that asketh receiveth; and he that seeketh findeth; and to him that knocketh it shall be opened (Luke 11:9-10).

Excerpt: *Release Your Anointing Expanded Edition*, Chapter 2.

Jesus said that those who seek shall find. Jesus wants us to desire the Holy Ghost. Would you ask for something and have your head or hand turned the other way? Jesus wants our hearts to be lined up with what our lips are saying.

Jesus taught this parable:

. . .what woman having ten pieces of silver, if she lose one piece, doth not light a candle, and sweep the house, and seek diligently till she find it? And when she hath found it, she calleth her friends and her neighbours together, saying, Rejoice with me; for I have found the piece which I had lost (Luke 15:8-9).

When this woman realized she didn't have her precious coin, she lit a candle, swept the house, and searched diligently until she found it. We must be in the same place of earnest seeking in regard to the Holy Ghost.

We must sweep our house and purge ourselves of anything that isn't of God. Then we must seek the Holy Ghost diligently. We must earnestly want the Holy Ghost and refuse to compromise. You can be real and have the Holy Ghost. It isn't something mysterious. This is God's will for your life!

Your Thoughts

I. What has Luke 11:9-10 meant to you personally? What have you sought for spiritually? What have you found that gives meaning to these words?

_____

_____

_____

_____

_____

2. Have you ever lost something valuable and become determined to continue looking until you found it? What makes the lost object worth the struggle and time to find it? Is the Holy Ghost this valuable to you?

_____

_____

_____

3. Why do you think people often ask for something and turn away before receiving it? What position do we need to be in so we receive the blessings of God, including the Holy Spirit?

_____

_____

4. What counsel would you give someone who wanted to know how to receive the baptism of the Holy Ghost? What can you share from your personal experience? What can you share from the principles in Scripture?

_____

_____

5. In your opinion, how does diligence come to play in regard to seeking the Holy Spirit? What kinds of compromise could we entertain so we do not really receive the Holy Spirit?

_____

_____

_____

_____

_____

_____

Meditation

"God rewards those who diligently seek Him (see Heb. 11:6). *Diligently* means to be stretched out for that which you are asking. The Holy Ghost, His power, and the change that He alone can bring in your life must be so precious that you will not accept a counterfeit. Nothing else will suffice."

Is your heart focused with a desire that will not take no for an answer? Do you really want the power of the Holy Ghost?

DAY 9

YOU HAVE TO KNOCK!

If ye then, being evil, know how to give good gifts unto your children: **how much more** *shall your heavenly Father give the Holy Spirit to them that ask Him?* (Luke 11:13)

Excerpt: *Release Your Anointing Expanded Edition*, Chapter 2.

Those who want the power of the Holy Ghost must take a three-step approach: *ask, seek,* and *knock*. What prompts you to open your front door? When someone knocks, you see who it is and what they want.

Jesus said to knock. Before knocking, you must have a desire to ask. This driving desire caused you to come to the door with great expectation and determination. You searched until you found the door—and now you knock.

It may seem that Jesus has these steps out of order, but that's not true. If you have no will to ask, there's no reason to knock. Without the will to seek, there's no reason to knock. Knocking is preceded by a will to ask and search diligently. Knocking gives you access to what you have diligently sought.

An earthly father can be very biased. Sometimes he is stubborn, and sometimes he gives for all the wrong reasons. Jesus made it very clear: If the child asks for one thing, the Father will not give another.

The emphasis in Luke 11:13 (see above) is on "how much more."

Take the Word as authoritative—ask, seek, knock.

Your Thoughts

1. The author describes a three-step approach to receiving the power of the Holy Ghost. Think through each of the steps and define them in terms of your own knowledge and experience.

_____

_____

2. How does your desire to ask for the Holy Ghost precede your coming to God to "knock" for His empowerment? How much does asking have to do with your attitude and eagerness to receive?

_____

_____

_____

3. How is your will involved in the three steps of asking, seeking, and knocking? What does a person's will have to do with the determination to receive?

---

4. If children ask for something good that is within your power to give, do you find it pleasurable and easy to give them what they ask? Why does it please us to give to a youngster? How does this example show us why the Father seeks to give blessings to us?

---

5. Explain Luke 11:13 in your own words, emphasizing the experience that you have with the progression explained in the verse. What are some things God may want you to ask, seek, and knock for right now?

_____

_____

_____

_____

_____

Meditation

"God knows that we need the power of the Holy Ghost. Spiritual gifts function only as the Holy Ghost empowers the child of God. As you ask and seek, remember that God knows your motives. He endues you with the power of the Holy Ghost to give you victory over satan, to make you joyful, and to enable you to function in the gifts of the Spirit."

Why do spiritual gifts only function when the Holy Ghost empowers us? Have you experienced this type of empowerment? Do you operate in it on a daily basis?

DAY 10

THE POWER AND ARMY OF THE HOLY GHOST

The wind bloweth where it listeth, and thou hearest the sound thereof, but canst not tell whence it cometh, and whither it goeth: so is every one that is born of the Spirit (John 3:8).

Excerpt: *Release Your Anointing Expanded Edition,* Chapter 2.

The power of the Holy Spirit can make you everything God said you could be. Adam illustrates this perfectly. The Bible says that Adam was only a form until God breathed on him (see Gen. 2:7). Only then did Adam become a living soul.

Until God breathed on him Adam had potential but no power. God breathed into Adam the power to reach his potential. The mere form of man became a living soul.

And suddenly there came a sound from Heaven as of a rushing mighty wind, and it filled all the house where they were sitting (Acts 2:2).

You have great potential. With great potential comes great responsibility. God has shaped you, but you need His power to become everything He desires for you to become. Without the power of the Holy Ghost you can go to Heaven, but you will never reach your potential. Your ministry, gifts, calling, life, and your marriage will be only a form of what it could have been.

Without a word from God the valley of dry bones that Ezekiel saw would have never been raised to form an army.

Look at the principles from Ezekiel 37:

1. You must be willing to confess your condition.

2. You must confess that you are merely a form of what you could be.

3. You must hear the Word of God.

4. The Word will bring about change.

5. The potential will be realized as the Word brought about the wind.

Your Thoughts

1. Have you felt God's mighty wind in your life? If your life is calm, where do you think God can stir it up with His breath of life?

_____

_____

2. In the busyness of your days, do you take enough time to feel His cool breeze of refreshment? What steps can you take to set aside time to walk in His presence?

_____

_____

3. Do you sense hidden potential within your spirit? Is there a career or ministry that seems "right" for you to pursue? What's holding you back?

_____

_____

_____

4. Do you ever feel powerless regarding family situations, ministry problems, career challenges? Why haven't you tapped into the power of the Holy Ghost to help you through these situations?

_____

_____

_____

5. Ezekiel saw dry bones come to life with a word from God. How important is the Word of God in your daily life? Are there words He is speaking to you through His Word the Bible that gives you the power to conquer any and every problem?

_____

_____

_____

_____

_____

Meditation

"The Word came from the four corners of the earth. That tells me that there isn't an area that God cannot fill with the Holy Ghost—your past, your childhood, your feelings of inferiority, your wounds, your loneliness. The Holy Ghost can fill you from the north, south, east, and west."

Do you believe that within you is an army? No matter what others say, God sees incredible potential in you. You merely need to dispel satan's fear and allow the wind to breathe upon that which God has formed in you. Say a prayer now that it be so.

DAY II

PENTECOST HAS
FULLY COME

And when the day of Pentecost was fully come, they were all with one accord in one place. And suddenly there cam a sound from Heaven as of a rushing mighty wind, and it filled all the house where they were sitting. And there appeared unto them cloven tongues like as of fire, and it sat upon each of them. And they were all filled with the Holy Ghost, and began to speak with other tongues, as the Spirit gave them utterance (Acts 2:1-4).

Excerpt: *Release Your Anointing Expanded Edition*, Chapter 3.

The Jews were familiar with the term Pentecost. Everything God did in types and shadows in the Old Testament was fulfilled in the New Testament. In the Old Testament God revealed Himself in many ways to Israel. He was known as the "I Am," promising to sustain them on their journey from Egypt to Canaan.

Pentecost was a type of something that one day would explode and change this world for eternity. Everything that needed to precede Pentecost had taken place. Jesus, the Passover Lamb, had died and risen from the dead. He had walked with His disciples, was confirmed 40 days and nights with many infallible proofs, and then was received into glory.

Our personal Passover must precede our Pentecost. The blood of Christ prepares us for Pentecost, washing away our sin and prejudice, enabling us to come together with devout men and women from every nation.

Your Thoughts

I. Jesus was the *true* bread from Heaven (see John 6:32). Do we receive Jesus as food from Heaven? Do we realize that God gave us Jesus to sustain our lives physically, mentally, emotionally, and spiritually? How do you acknowledge this ultimate gift?

_____

_____

_____

_____

_____

_____

2. Have you allowed the blood of Christ to prepare you for Pentecost? Have your sins and prejudice been washed away?

_____

_____

_____

3. Are you guilty of devising a grading scale to judge the severity of certain sins of others? How about your own sins?

_____

_____

_____

4. God is tearing down racial, ethnic, and religious barriers to reach the entire world for Christ. Are you doing the same within your realm of influence?

_____

_____

_____

5. How can you better prepare yourself for your personal Passover that precedes your Pentecost experience?

_____

_____

_____

_____

_____

_____

Meditation

"Pentecost marked the beginning of a mission for the Jews as they gathered in the fruit of their labors. Pentecost in Acts chapter 2 marks the beginning of a mission for the church to gather in lost souls. We need Pentecost to fully arise in our lives as we fall in love with Jesus, the Passover Lamb, to carry out the ingathering of His harvest."

Have you experienced a personal Pentecost experience? In what ways has it changed your perspective of life? Are you willing to share that experience with others?

DAY 12

WHY TONGUES?

In the law it is written, With men of other tongues and other lips will I speak unto this people; and yet for all that will they not hear Me, saith the Lord. Wherefore tongues are for a sign, not to them that believe, but to them that believe not: but prophesying serveth not for them that believe not, but for them which believe (1 Corinthians 14:21-22).

Excerpt: *Release Your Anointing Expanded Edition,* Chapter 3.

God chose tongues as a sign of the Holy Spirit for a significant reason. He took the most difficult, uncontrollable member of our body and caused it to yield to divinely inspired speech. Bridling the tongue may be impossible for us to do in our own strength, but the supernatural outpouring of the Holy Ghost enabled the disciples to use their tongues for the purposes of God—and it will do the same for us.

Speaking in tongues can occur in two different settings. A believer may pray in tongues privately to commune with God (see 1 Cor. 14:2,4).

Scripture also teaches on the gift of tongues or *"divers* [different] *kinds of tongues"* (I Cor. 12:10), which is used in a public assembly.

When the gift of tongues is given in a public assembly, the message needs to be interpreted for the hearers to benefit (see I Cor. 14:27). Sometimes, as on the day of Pentecost, the gift of tongues is given to minister to the hearers in their own language (see Acts 2:6).

Isn't it amazing that men can hear the manifestation of the Holy Ghost but fail to believe? Mockers concluded, *"These men are full of new wine"* (Acts 2:13).

Your Thoughts

1. How easy is it for you to control your tongue? Do you find it to be, as James 3:2-8 says, something that is *"untamable"*?

    _____

    _____

2. Have you experienced praying in tongues privately to commune with God? What use does this ability have in the life of a believer?

    _____

    _____

3. Have you or someone you know received the gift of
    tongues for public assemblies? Why does this gift
    need to be accompanied by an interpretation of the
    tongue?

    _____

    _____

    _____

    _____

4. If you had been in the crowd on the Day of
    Pentecost after Jesus' ascension, what would you have
    thought if you had heard your native tongue being
    spoken by an unlearned fisherman? Why do you
    think the people responded by thinking the disciples
    were drunk?

    _____

    _____

    _____

    _____

    _____

5. Since the ability to pray in tongues is a sign of receiving the Holy Spirit, why do you think it is important that we all speak in tongues, as Paul says in First Corinthians 14:5? We should not look at this legalistically, but why should this experience be greatly encouraged for all believers?

_____

_____

_____

_____

Meditation

"When we are filled with the Holy Ghost, He acts as a deterrent. He places a bit in our mouths and bridles our speech. Just when you feel like telling someone off, the Holy Ghost takes control. Isn't it exciting that God took the tongue, a member of our body known for being "a fire, a world of iniquity," and sanctified it for His purposes?"

Have you experienced the Holy Spirit's power to bridle your tongue when you were about to say something that was not godly? How can we increase our ability to have the Holy Spirit control out tongue throughout our daily lives?

DAY 13

THE REFINER'S FIRE

I indeed baptize you with water unto repentance: but He that cometh after me is mightier than I, whose shoes I am not worthy to bear: He shall baptize you with the Holy Ghost, and with fire: Whose fan is in His hand, and He will thoroughly purge His floor, and gather His wheat into the garner; but He will burn up the chaff with unquenchable fire (Matthew 3:11-12).

Excerpt: *Release Your Anointing Expanded Edition*, Chapter 3.

Fire will not destroy gold, but fire purifies gold. When God polishes His gold, He uses fiery trials. Unfortunately, nothing brings luster to your character and commitment to your heart like opposition does. The finished product is a result of the fiery process. Whenever you see someone shining with the kind of brilliancy that enables God to look down and see Himself, you are looking at someone who has been through the furnace of affliction.

Let me warn you: God places His prize possessions in the fire. The bad news is, even those who live godly lives will suffer persecution. The good news is, you might be in the fire, but God controls the thermostat! He knows how hot it needs to be to accomplish His purpose in your life.

His hand has fanned the flames that were needed to teach patience, prayer, and many other invaluable lessons. We don't enjoy them, but we need them. What a joy to know that He cares enough to straighten out the jagged places in our lives. It is His fatherly corrections that confirm us as legitimate children—not illegitimate ones. He affirms my position in Him by correcting and chastening me.

Your Thoughts

I. If you are God's investment of gold, does it stand to reason that He would want to have the purest gold possible? How does His desire for purity within us benefit us?

_____

_____

_____

_____

_____

_____

2. Have you ever been through a fiery process that you knew was God's refining fire in your life? If so, how did this process work to take out the impurities in your character?

_____

_____

_____

_____

3. Name someone who shines as brilliant pure gold, reflecting the Father. What characteristics do they have that make them seem so pure to you? What kinds of trials might they have gone through to receive that purity?

_____

_____

_____

_____

_____

4. Knowing that God has control of the thermostat during our purification can give us comfort. Why? How does trusting Him during the process of refinement help us see past the immediate pain?

_____

_____

_____

_____

5. What are some areas of your life that God is purifying right now? How does His Fatherhood come to bear when He places you in the fire? Why do we need this process?

_____

_____

_____

_____

Meditation

"It is impossible to discuss the value of investing in people and not find ourselves worshiping God—what a perfect picture of investment. God is the major stockholder.…. The greatest primary investment He made was the inflated, unthinkable price of redemption that He paid. What He did on the Cross was worship. Normally the lesser worships the greater, but this time, the greater worshiped the lesser. What an investment!"

How has God made an investment in you? How have you made an investment in others? Do you think God sees your investment in other people as an act of worship?

DAY 14

HIS INVESTMENT

Verily, verily, I say unto you, Except a corn of wheat fall into the ground and die, it abideth alone: but if it die, it bringeth forth much fruit (John 12:24).

Excerpt: *Release Your Anointing Expanded Edition*, Chapter 3.

God has an investment in our lives. First of all, no one invests without the expectation of gain. The apostle Paul wrote, *"But we have this treasure in earthen vessels, that the excellency of the power may be of God, and not of us,"* (2 Cor. 4:7). Thus, according to Scripture, we possess treasure. However, the excellency of what we have is not of us, but of God. The treasure is *of* God. It is accumulated in us and then presented back to Him.

We are fertile ground—broken by troubles, enriched by failures, and watered with tears. Yet undeniably there is a deposit within us. This deposit is valuable enough to place us on satan's hit list. Paul prayed that *"the eyes of your understanding being enlightened..."* (Eph. 1:18). Paul challenged them to become progressively aware of the enormity of His inheritance in us, not our inheritance in Him. We spend most of our time talking about what we want from God. The real issue is what He wants from us. It is the Lord who has the greatest investment. We are the parched, dry ground from which Christ springs. Believe me, God is serious about His investment!

Your Thoughts

1. If no one invests without the expectation of gain, how would God Almighty, who has all resources, decide to invest for His gain? What gain do you think God sees in us to prove His investment in us is wise?

_____

_____

_____

2. What treasure has God placed inside you? What spiritual fruit has been seen by others within your life? What gifts have you employed? What kind of positive character traits have you used for God's glory?

_____

_____

_____

3. What makes a person have *fertile ground*? What has produced fertile ground in your life? Do you think you are ready and fertile for God's investment today?

_____

_____

_____

_____

_____

4. The deposit God has made places us on satan's hit list. Have you sensed this threat at any time in your life? Why does satan dislike the deposit within us? What is his strategy for stopping God's investment from maturing to great gain?

_____

_____

_____

_____

_____

5. Why should we be talking more about what *God* wants from us than what *we* want from God? In your opinion, how does God view His inheritance in you?

_____

_____

_____

_____

_____

Meditation

"It has been suggested that if you walk in the Spirit, you won't have to contend with the fire. Real faith doesn't mean you won't go through the fire, however. Real faith simply means that when you pass through the fire, He will be with you. This thought brings you to an unusual reality.... The presence of the Lord can turn a burning inferno into a walk in the park!"

Have you ever felt disillusionment because you thought you could escape trials once you became a Christian? How have real trials helped you sense God's presence? Are there current trials that have revealed to you your need to sense God's presence?

DAY 15

FAITH

Quenched the violence of fire, escaped the edge of the sword, out of weakness were made strong, waxed valiant in fight, turned to flight the armies of the aliens (Hebrews 11:34).

Excerpt: *Release Your Anointing Expanded Edition*, Chapter 3.

Hebrews chapter 11 discusses at length the definition of faith. It then shares the deeds of faith in verses 32-35a, and finally it discusses the perseverance of faith in verses 35b-39. There are distinctions of faith as well. In Hebrews 11:32-35a, the teaching has placed an intensified kind of emphasis on the distinct faith that escapes peril and overcomes obstacles.

However, in the verses that end the chapter, the writer deals with the distinctions of another kind of faith. In his closing remarks, he shares that there were some other believers whose faith was exemplified *through* suffering and not *from* suffering (see Heb. 11:36-37).

Christianity's foundation is not built on elite mansions, stocks and bonds, or sports cars and cruise-control living. The Church is built on the backs of men and women who withstood discomfort for a cause. These people were not the end but the means whereby God was glorified. Some of them exhibited their faith through their shadows' healing sick people. Still others exhibited their faith by bleeding to death beneath piles of stone. They also had a brand of faith that seemed to ease the effect, though it didn't alter the cause.

Your Thoughts

I. Define faith in your own words. How does your definition compare or contrast with the one given in Hebrews chapter 11?

_____

_____

_____

2. What is the difference between deeds that are done by us as we strive in our power and will versus those that are done by faith? Do you have examples of these from your own life?

_____

_____

_____

3. How do you think someone "perseveres" in faith? How does perseverance help grow our faith? What makes our faith distinct so we can escape peril and overcome obstacles?

_____

_____

_____

_____

_____

4. How is faith exemplified *through* suffering? How does this type of faith encourage other believers? How does it bring a witness to the world?

_____

_____

_____

_____

_____

5. What do you think the following means: "These people were not the end but the means whereby God was glorified"? Are you an example of faith to those around you? Does your faith bring glory to God?

_____

_____

_____

_____

_____

Meditation

"As the fire of persecution forces us to make deeper levels of commitment, it is so important that our faith be renewed to match our level of commitment. There is a place in God where the fire consumes every other desire but to know the Lord in the power of His resurrection. At this level all other pursuits tarnish and seem worthless in comparison."

How do you renew your faith? What process do you go through? How can you be prepared to face persecution through your growth in faith?

DAY 16

SECRET CODE

Surely the Lord God will do nothing, but He revealeth His secret unto his servants the prophets (Amos 3:7).

Excerpt: *Release Your Anointing Expanded Edition,* Chapter 4.

God has spoken to His people from the very beginning (see Gen. 3:8). God spoke to His people through the prophets (see Heb. 1:1). He also spoke to us by His Son (see Heb.1:2). He spoke to us by miracles (see Heb.2:4). He then spoke by His apostles. As a result of the mighty outpouring at Pentecost, God said He would speak through His Spirit (see Joel 2:28).

God is speaking a vital message in these last days. He is looking for someone to deliver a timely, life-changing word. Many times, however, it is in secret code and can only be understood by those who have the Holy Ghost.

When God speaks in secret, He does so for at least two reasons:

1. God wants to have an intimate relationship with you. You tell your secrets and innermost thoughts only to your closest, most trusted friends.

2. By speaking in secret code, God insures that the devil does not understand the strategy of the church. This enables us to make an unannounced surprise attack because the secret code bypasses the radar and defense system of the satanic forces in opposition to us (see Eph. 6:12).

Your Thoughts

I. Think through the ways God has revealed Himself in the Old Testament. To whom did He speak face to face? Do you know examples of Old Testament people who heard God speak? What were some of the situations when this communication took place?

_____

_____

_____

_____

_____

_____

2. How do we know that Jesus spoke only the Words of
    the Father? Why do you think people so easily
    received His words? Why were there so many who
    did not receive?

    _____

    _____

    _____

3. What are some examples of when God spoke
    through the apostles? Highlight things you remember
    He told us through them.

    _____

    _____

    _____

4. How can you be sure that God really wants to speak
    important messages to us today? What do you think
    you need to do to be in the receiving position to
    hear Him?

    _____

    _____

5. As God speaks in secret code, why doesn't satan understand what He says? How does it make you feel to understand that God speaks with His most trusted friends?

_____

_____

_____

_____

Meditation

"Many try to limit God, saying He has spoken in the past but has ceased to speak today. This, however, is not true....

"The Holy Ghost also speaks to us today. Tongues are God's message for the last days. It isn't the only way that He can speak, but it is one avenue of speech. We need faith to allow Him to speak and interpret the message through a willing vessel."

We may believe that others have limited God because they do not believe in the gifts He still gives to us today. But first we may need to look at the log in our own eyes. Take time before the Lord and ask Him to reveal to you if there have been times when you lacked the faith to allow Him to speak to you more intimately.

DAY 17

MYSTERIES OF THE KINGDOM

If ye love Me, keep My commandments. And I will pray the Father, and He shall give you another Comforter, that He may abide with you for ever; Even the Spirit of truth; whom the world cannot receive, because it seeth Him not, neither knoweth Him: but ye know Him; for He dwelleth with you, and shall be in you (John 14:15-17).

Excerpt: *Release Your Anointing Expanded Edition*, Chapter 4.

This Scripture indicates the Kingdom of God was going through some drastic changes.

1. We find the changing of the guard. *"I will pray the Father, and he shall give you another Comforter"* (vs. 16).

2. We find an obligation on our part to receive the Holy Ghost. Jesus said, *"If Ye love me, keep My commandments"* (vs. 15). As a result of our obedience, Jesus said that He would pray to the Father. He in turn would send another Comforter to us.

3. Jesus said three things about the Holy Ghost in John 14:17:

- The world cannot receive Him.

- The world cannot see Him, because His ways are not their ways; He is a mystery to them.

- The world doesn't know Him.

All the miracles of Christ declared what His followers would do in that day. Because the world did not receive Him, did not see Him, and did not know Him, they crucified the Lord of glory.

God calls those who are committed to excellence to a place of seclusion and aloneness. The Holy Ghost is saying, "Detach yourself from things that blind you from seeing My mysteries and deafen you from hearing My language."

Your Thoughts

1. In your own words, summarize the ways that John 14:15-17 shows that the Kingdom of God was going through some drastic changes. How were these changes important to what would happen following Christ's ascension?

_____

_____

_____

2. Why are we "obliged" to receive the Holy Ghost? Why is this obligation more than a mere choice? If Jesus said He would pray for us to receive the Holy Ghost, how should we pray?

    _____

    _____

    _____

3. How does receiving the Holy Ghost separate us from the world? In what ways is this an opportunity for the world to look to us, the Church, as a source of healing for them?

    _____

    _____

4. How do the miracles that Jesus performed show us what we are to do? Think through some of those miracles and list some. Are these part of our current job description?

    _____

    _____

5. How does seclusion and aloneness bring us to a
    place of excellence? How do times of retreat help
    blind our eyes to the world and open our ears to the
    Holy Ghost?

_____

_____

_____

_____

Meditation

"Jesus is speaking, but even those in the Church are missing
Him because they do not hear His language. Many are not hearing His voice because tradition has left them content with only the
first glimpse of His glory. The glory of Christ far exceeds any
glory ever known by man. In those three short years Jesus began to
reveal the mysteries of a powerful Kingdom that was greater than
any problem, sickness, or dilemma."

In what ways do you think the Church is missing what Jesus is
speaking? What mysteries does He desire to share with the Church
that will help His Kingdom in these last days? Are you available to
hear these mysteries? Why or why not?

DAY 18

LIGHT AND SALT

You are the salt of the earth: but if the salt has lost his savour, where-with shall it be salted? It is thenceforth good for nothing, but to be cast out, and to be trodden under foot of men (Matthew 5:13).

Excerpt: *Release Your Anointing Expanded Edition*, Chapter 4.

As the Church allows the Holy Ghost to work in and through us, the world will begin to see Jesus and the Kingdom of God in action. It will be a mystery to the world but a powerful reality to the Church. But it won't happen overnight. It's progressive, day by day, trial by trial, storm by storm, valley by valley, and temptation by temptation.

When Jesus was on earth, He said, *"I am the light of the world: he that followeth Me shall not walk in darkness, but shall have the light of life"* (John 8:12).

But when He died, darkness covered the earth. Except for the Holy Ghost, darkness will prevail.

We are beacons, lighthouses to a world of storm-tossed, beaten, battered individuals. We are to be a city set on a hill and illuminated by the Holy Ghost. Our joy, peace, righteousness should shine brightly, encouraging others to find refuge in our God. The fruit of the Spirit in our lives acts as a magnet to draw them to Jesus.

Salt does several things: creates thirst, preserves, burns wounds, and seasons.

Your Thoughts

1. Are you a lighthouse in a dark world? Is your light flickering in the window or shining brightly from the rooftop?

   _____

   _____

   _____

2. Are you seasoning those around you with the taste of God's grace and mercy? If not, what are some ways in which you can spread His seasoning to friends and family?

   _____

   _____

   _____

3. Are your joy, peace, and righteousness shining for all to see? Do you think it is important for Christians to be a beacon of light to others—even if they don't "feel" like it?

_____

_____

_____

_____

_____

4. Have you given the Holy Ghost permission to saturate your very being with His salt and light so you can then pass it on to sad and desperate people around you?

_____

_____

_____

_____

_____

5. Allowing God to use you as salt and light fulfills your God-given destiny.

_____

_____

_____

_____

_____

_____

_____

Meditation

"When Jesus walked the earth, He was a preservative for the world. A thief could not die without first being preserved by His forgiveness (see Luke 23:42); a widow's only son, the apple of her eye, could not reach the gates of death with Jesus stopping the funeral procession (see Luke 7:12). Lazarus could not lay decomposing in a tomb without hearing a voice, '*Lazarus, come forth!*' (John 11:43)."

Are you preserving, stopping, calling, shining?

DAY 19

GOD HAS YOUR NUMBER

The people that do know their God shall be strong, and do exploits (Daniel 11:32).

Excerpt: *Release Your Anointing Expanded Edition*, Chapter 4.

God is ringing your telephone today. He may have to call you to give you a message for someone else, who for one reason or another, cannot hear. The only way the message can get through is for you to speak out what God has spoken into your spirit. Be sure to pray for an interpreter.

Many anointed people wrongly believe that their anointing gives them the right to get out of order. They may exercise their gift, but the message of God is misrepresented, wrong, or even damaging. This confuses and wounds people.

And the spirits of the prophets are subject to the prophets (I Corinthians 14:32).

Timeliness is an important issue with the gift of tongues. Your anointing may not always be in dispute as much as your timing. If your message is not given in its proper timing, it can hurt, confuse, and mislead. The Holy Spirit is not unseemly. He does not cause disorder.

God is looking for a Church who believes He can confirm them and their ministry with gifts, signs, and wonders in the Holy Ghost. (See Hebrews 2:3-4 and Mark 16:17-18.)

Your Thoughts

1. Have you ever experienced receiving a message that was not for you only? How does God work in this way? Why does He do so?

_____

_____

2. In what ways can people justify being out of order because they have received a message from God for others? When we get a message for others, we have a responsibility not only to deliver it in purity, but to deliver it when God asks us to do so. Why?

_____

_____

_____

3. What does submission have to do with the public use of any gift? Who are we to be submitted to in Heaven and on earth? Why?

_____

_____

_____

_____

_____

4. How can the mistake of not being timely with your gifts work against your anointing? When someone in authority does not receive your gift, what should you do?

_____

_____

_____

_____

_____

5. If God wants to entrust us with His ministry gifts, how can we prepare ourselves to learn timeliness and submission before we "train wreck" the expression of those gifts? If our hearts are right, what else needs to be right so we do not hurt, confuse, or mislead others?

_____

_____

_____

_____

Meditation

"Don't be dismayed if those who see you say, 'These people are fanatics!' The Holy Ghost will cause a division between truth and falsehood. When you begin to function in the gift of God for your life and the devil sees a true manifestation of the Holy Ghost, expect to be put on the devil's hit list. This is nothing more than a trick of the enemy to get you to stop."

Honestly think through your feelings if other people thought you were a fanatic because you spoke in tongues. Why would such a division be expected? What do you need to do to prepare your emotions and your spirit if you are rejected because of your beliefs?

DAY 20

MESSAGES FROM HEAVEN

Eye hath not seen, nor ear heard, neither have entered into the heart of man, the things which God hath prepared for them that love him. But God hath revealed them unto us by his Spirit: for the Spirit searcheth all things, yea, the deep things of God (I Corinthians 2:9-10).

Excerpt: *Release Your Anointing Expanded Edition,* Chapter 4.

Let's look at seven areas of your life in which the Holy Ghost wants to speak.

1. The Holy Ghost wants to speak to you things that go beyond human logic, natural tendency, and physical comprehension (see I Cor. 2:9-10).

2. The Holy Ghost will testify to you (see Rom. 8:16).

3. The Holy Ghost will give you direction (see Acts 8:29). Sometimes the message is for yourself, others give direction.

4. The Holy Ghost speaks to lead us to obedience (see Acts 10:1-23).

5. The Holy Ghost shows you God's choice for companionship (see Acts 13:2).

6. The Holy Ghost will speak and close doors that were the right thing but the wrong time (see Acts 16:6-7).

7. The Holy Ghost sometimes warns us (see Acts 21:4).

The Holy Ghost speaks for a variety of reasons. His word may be for you or someone else. He may testify to your spirit of God's faithfulness.

Instead of questions for Your Thoughts,
think through the seven areas and fill out the following chart.

AREA	SCRIPTURAL EXAMPLE Who, what, where, when, how, why	PERSONAL EXAMPLE
1.		
2.		
3.		
4.		

(chart continued)

AREA	SCRIPTURAL EXAMPLE Who, what, where,	PERSONAL EXAMPLE
5.		
6.	_____	
7.	_____	

Meditation

"God is trying to intervene in your life. He may use you to intervene in the life of someone who may not be answering His call. Whatever the case, you can be confident that it is right because our *parakletos*, the Holy Ghost, speaks only the counsel He has heard in Heaven."

How do you think God is trying to intervene in your life? Why is your confidence important to be able to use the gifts that God has given to you? How does it make you feel to know that you can receive the counsel of Heaven?

DAY 21

THE TRANSFORMER

But as many as received Him, to them gave He power to become the sons of God, even to them that believe on His name (John 1:12).

Excerpt: *Release Your Anointing Expanded Edition*, Chapter 5.

I pray that we as Christians never lose our conviction that God does change lives. We must protect this message. Our God enables us to make the radical changes necessary for fulfilling our purposes and responsibilities. Like the caterpillar that eats and sleeps its way into change, the process occurs gradually, but nonetheless powerfully. Many people who will rock this world are sleeping in the cocoon of obscurity, waiting for their change to come. The Scriptures declare, "*...it is high time to awake out of sleep: for now is our salvation nearer than when we believed*" (Rom. 13:11).

God made the *first* transformer! He created man from dust. He created him in such a way that, if need be, He could pull a woman out of him without ever having to reach back into the dust. Out of one creative act God transformed the man into a marriage. Then He transformed the marriage into a family, the family into a society. God never had to reach into the ground again because the power to transform was intrinsically placed into man. All types of potential were locked into our spirits before birth.

For the Christian, transformation at its optimum is the outworking of the internal. God placed certain things in us that must come out. We house the prophetic power of God. Every word of our personal prophetic destiny is inside us. He has ordained us to be!

Your Thoughts

1. How strong is your conviction that God does change lives? Have you seen evidence of this among the people in your spiritual family? Why is this conviction important to our ability to change?

_____

_____

_____

2. What do you think God is doing as people remain in obscurity waiting for their time to rock the world? How does progressive change work in your life?

_____

_____

3. God's business of transformation began with Adam. Think through all the possibilities God placed in Adam—what are some of these possibilities? What possibilities do you think God placed within you?

_____

_____

_____

_____

_____

4. Why does God put potential within our spirits before we are born? What does this potential have to do with our destiny in God's Kingdom?

_____

_____

_____

_____

_____

5. How does God make us aware of our potential? How does He give us experience and training to bring this potential to external fruition?

_____

_____

_____

_____

_____

Meditation

"You are empowered by God to reach and accomplish goals that transcend human limitations! It is important that every vessel God uses realize that he or she was able to accomplish what others could not only because God gave them the grace to do so. God works out the internal destinies of His children. He gives us the power to become who we are eternally and internally."

Have you felt empowered by God to accomplish more than you could on your own? How has God's grace worked in your life? Meditate on the ways He has given you power to become who you are eternally and internally.

DAY 22

ORCHESTRATING CHANGE

And be not conformed to this world: but be ye transformed by the renewing of your mind, that ye may prove what is that good, and acceptable, and perfect, will of God (Romans 12:2).

Excerpt: *Release Your Anointing Expanded Edition*, Chapter 5.

It would be a sad day for the unsaved if the Holy Spirit stopped convicting people and drawing them to the Savior. Let's look at His work in the world today:

According to the passage in Romans, the Holy Ghost has arrested you on three counts:

1. He has reproved your sin, which means to convict, to expose, to convince of a wrong, to tell a fault.

2. He convinces you of righteousness or a right standing with God. His goodness, not your own, saves you.

3. He will convince you of judgment, not only of your future encounter with God, but also of ungodly influences that cause you to sin.

The Holy Ghost wants to orchestrate change in your life. Because you have messed up, many of you believe your calling has been annulled. The devil is a liar, for *"the gifts and callings of God are without repentance"* (Rom. 11:29).

The Holy Ghost has come to convince and influence you to change. Dare to be different! Refuse to become a part of the mundane crowd going nowhere. Rise up and shake yourself. Find yourself a church that is reflecting change by the influence of the Holy Ghost.

Your Thoughts

1. How did the Holy Spirit draw you to the Savior? Is He currently working on any people within your sphere of relationships?

_____

_____

_____

_____

_____

_____

2. How has the Holy Ghost convicted you of sin? Have you ever been embarrassed when your sin was exposed? How has the Holy Spirit convinced you that you were wrong when you thought you were right?

    _____

    _____

    _____

3. What did you think when the Holy Spirit convinced you that without Jesus you would not be able to stand before God? How did He present righteousness to you so you could understand God's grace through Jesus?

    _____

    _____

    _____

4. How has the Holy Ghost convinced you that God's judgment is real? What are some of the ungodly influences that will bring sin to your life?

    _____

    _____

5. Why do you think God does not annul our callings when we have sinned so greatly? How hard is it to believe that you can change from whatever you have been to what God wants you to be?

_____

_____

_____

_____

Meditation

"Change is a gift from God.... The Bible calls change *repentance*. Repentance is God's gift to a struggling heart who wants to find himself. Without the Holy Spirit's help you can search and search and still not find repentance. One moment with the Spirit of God can lead you into a place of renewal that, on your own, you would not find or enjoy."

Why do you think it is difficult for most of us to process change? If repentance is at the root of change, do you think it becomes even more difficult? Why or why not? Ask the Lord to help you embrace change and repentance as much as you embrace blessing.

DAY 23

THE HOLY SPIRIT'S INFLUENCE

Nevertheless I tell you the truth; It is expedient for you that I go away: for if I go not away, the Comforter will not come to you; but if I depart, I will send Him unto you (John 16:7).

Excerpt: *Release Your Anointing Expanded Edition*, Chapter 5.

The Holy Spirit brings His influence in the following five areas:

1. The Holy Ghost sets the stage for the Word of God (see Gen. 1:2).

The Spirit did the preparatory work for the Word to give the command: "Let there be...."

2. The Holy Spirit's influence will separate and declare (see Gen. 1:4-8).

The Holy Spirit will separate certain things from you, set limitations, and declare your destiny.

3. The Holy Spirit wants to resurrect buried seeds in your life (see Gen. 1:11-12). The seeds were there, but they were obscured.

God formed man from dust. But man is merely a form of what he can be before the Holy Spirit breathes into him vibrancy and freshness of life.

4. The Holy Spirit wrestles with us to bring us to a deeper commitment.

We need the Holy Spirit to go before us, preparing people's hearts and minds for the Word. If the Holy Ghost truly comes upon you, He will change your life.

5. The Holy Spirit seeks a place to rest in authority (see Gen. 8:8-12).

As Jesus stood in the Jordan, the dove descended from Heaven, landed on Him, and His authority and anointing rested on Jesus.

Your Thoughts

1. In what ways has the Holy Ghost set the stage for God's Word in your life? Have you allowed the Holy Ghost to continuously prepare you to receive more of God's Word?

_____

_____

2. How has the Holy Spirit separated and declared things to you so you were clear on right and wrong, good and better? Have you experienced any limitations from the Holy Spirit? Has He declared your destiny?

_____

_____

_____

_____

3. Before you were a Christian you were like Adam, just a form of a person. How did the Holy Spirit breathe life into you so you could receive the salvation that comes from Jesus Christ? How did the seeds that were planted in you before you were born then come to life?

_____

_____

_____

_____

4. Have you ever felt as if you were wrestling with the Holy Spirit? Have you felt God pulling or tugging you forward but the boundaries of your comfort zone held you back? How does the Holy Ghost change us so we can grow into a deeper commitment with God?

_____

_____

_____

_____

5. What authority has the Holy Spirit rested upon your shoulders? When you receive divine authority, how can the Holy Spirit give the fullness needed to accomplish the responsibilities of that authority?

_____

_____

_____

_____

Meditation

"The Holy Spirit wants to resurrect buried seeds in your life (see Gen. 1:11-12). The seeds were there, but they were obscured. God brought forth creatures from the waters (see Gen. 1:20). They were there, but the Word brought them forth from what had covered them. God commanded the earth to bring forth living creatures (see Gen. 1:24). They were there, but simply had to be brought forth."

How excited would you be if you suddenly inherited a stash of gold or priceless jewels from a distant relative? Do you think this same excitement could be yours as the Spirit moves and the Word reveals your God-given destiny? Would there be excitement in Heaven as well?

DAY 24

GOD MINES FOR GOLD

But He knoweth the way that I take; when He hath tried me, I shall come forth as gold (Job 23:10).

Excerpt: *Release Your Anointing Expanded Edition*, Chapter 5.

Job endured tremendous emotional pain and physical affliction. His troubles were not only known to God but were allowed by God. Losing his sons and daughters and possessions left Job feeling very much alone.

Every gold mine is hidden beneath the earth. Mining priceless jewels takes years of painstaking labor. Tons of earth must be removed.

In the same way, a gold mine is buried beneath your flesh. Crucifying your flesh is excruciating, but it must occur to reveal the gifts within you. Give God digging rights. After all, the mine belongs to Him.

Your Thoughts

1. How deep are your jewels hidden? Will it take years
    to uncover them, or will you allow the Holy Ghost
    to blow away the earth with His breath of life?

    _____

    _____

    _____

    _____

2. Have you given God the digging rights to your gold
    mine? Take an active step right now to sign over all
    rights to Him.

    _____

    _____

    _____

    _____

    _____

3. What jewels and gifts do you think are waiting to be discovered within you? Have you purposely allowed them to lay dormant? Why?

_____

_____

_____

_____

4. While you are hoping to expose your jewels and gifts, satan is hoping to keep them hidden. Do you ever feel weary from the battle?

_____

_____

_____

_____

_____

5. How can prayer ease the fatigue and lessen the hurt from battle scars?

_____

_____

_____

_____

_____

_____

Meditation

"The devil knows you're a gold mine waiting to be claimed and mined. Your adversary has covered your priceless jewels with your past, unconfessed sins, emotional traumas, and religious tradition. Little does the devil know that you have been buried alive. You merely need the Spirit to move, and the Word uncovers you. You are Heaven's best kept secret and hell's worst nightmare."

Allowing the Holy Spirit to move within us will defeat satan and foil his attempts to keep our jewels hidden. Pray for the Spirit to move mightily.

DAY 25

WHEN WINNING IS LOSING

Therefore leaving the principles of the doctrine of Christ, let us go on unto perfection; not laying again the foundation of repentance from dead works, and of faith toward God, Of the doctrine of baptisms, and of laying on of hands, and of resurrection of the dead, and of eternal judgment. And this will we do, if God permit (Hebrews 6:1-3).

Excerpt: *Release Your Anointing Expanded Edition*, Chapter 5.

As the Holy Spirit strives with you to bring you into submission and obedience, you may be holding on to the very thing that He wants. As you walk away you may feel as though you've won, but you've actually lost.

Some of you have matured, and the Holy Spirit wants to take you higher. But it's a choice. God asks you to push away from the familiar into the supernatural. People resist change, but in order to get to where God wants us—and to arrive on time—you must push away.

The Holy Spirit flew on missions in the Old Testament as He rested on Abraham, Isaac, and Jacob, but they were not the one.

Finally, He looked from the portals of glory and saw the One. There was only One found worthy in Heaven and earth for the dove to land upon—Jesus.

When Jesus was dying, He said, *"Father, into thy hands I commend* [put into your trust] *my spirit"* (Luke 23:46). This same dove swept down from glory as a mighty rushing wind (see Acts 2:2). He found a body, the Church, to inhabit and to rest His authority upon.

Your Thoughts

I. How does the Holy Spirit bring you to submission and obedience? What methods does He use to get your attention and convince you to make a change?

_____

_____

_____

_____

_____

_____

2. Rate your maturity over the last five years. Has the Holy Spirit taken you on a steady progression of growth? Have there been peaks and valleys in the continuum of your maturing?

_____

_____

3. Why do we have to push away from something in order to receive change and get to where God wants us? Does this show how our will is involved in change? What does timing have to do with change?

_____

_____

_____

4. Review how the Holy Spirit worked in the lives of Old Testament heroes and New Testament apostles. What are some of the miracles they performed that seem completely out of their reach? How did the Holy Spirit work within them to change them?

_____

_____

5. As a member of the Church, you have been given the same Spirit that lived in Jesus. What does this awareness mean to you? Whose authority do you have?

_____

_____

_____

_____

_____

Meditation

"We can attain a place in God that is higher than our problems, giving us a divine perspective. We must be led to this place. It is against our nature to want this rock. We must oppose our flesh and say, 'When my spirit is overwhelmed, my spirit goes beyond nature and finds satisfaction only in the supernatural.' We ask God to lead us to the rock—Jesus—and away from earthly logic."

Have you ever experienced a mountaintop perspective on a situation or challenge? As you looked down from God's perspective, how did He change your attitude? How did He adjust your logic?

DAY 26

DO YOU WANT CHILDREN?

The Holy Ghost shall come upon thee, and the power of the Highest shall overshadow thee: therefore also that holy thing which shall be born of thee shall be called the Son of God (Luke 1:35).

Excerpt: *Release Your Anointing Expanded Edition*, Chapter 6.

Many Christians never conceive a child. Many do not want children because they do not want commitment and responsibility. Many have been impregnated by the Holy Ghost but have chosen to abort the baby. Other Christians who cannot carry their baby to term have miscarried.

The womb was designed as a receptacle for the seed of man and a place for a conceived child to develop. The Bible says Adam knew his wife (see Gen. 4:1,25). This intimate relationship gave them a son. You can trace the lineage of Christ back to the fruit of this first intimate relationship.

Mary was a virgin when the angel announced she would have a baby. She asked, *"How shall this be, seeing I know not a man?"* (Luke 1:34). This child was conceived by the power of the Holy Ghost.

Three things were to happen:

1. Conception—*"Thou shalt conceive"* (Luke 1:31).

2. Intimacy—"The Holy Ghost shall come upon thee."

3. Implanting of the Seed—"The power of the Highest shall overshadow thee."

It was totally the work of the Holy Ghost, but He had to have a womb in which to do His work.

Your Thoughts

1. Why is it so important that our intimacy with the Holy Spirit bears children? Why aren't we just permitted to have a honeymoon relationship that lasts for eternity?

   _____

   _____

   _____

   _____

   _____

   _____

2. When two people commit to the responsibility of biological children, what are the considerations they need to entertain? When we commit to the responsibility of spiritual children, what are the considerations we need to entertain?

    _____

    _____

    _____

3. What do you think it means to conceive spiritual children? What process might this take?

    _____

    _____

4. What does "intimacy with the Holy Ghost" mean to you? Does it have to do with *quantity* of time? Does it have to do with *quality* of time?

    _____

    _____

    _____

5. How does the "implanting of the seed" take place in terms of spiritual progeny? Why does the Holy Spirit have to be the One who does the implanting? What does it take for us to be ready for this event?

_____

_____

_____

_____

Meditation

"Many are afraid to fall in love with the Holy Ghost because they know that commitment brings intimacy, and intimacy brings conception, and conception brings labor, and labor produces a baby. As in the natural realm, it takes an intimate relationship to conceive.... [but] they do not want to endure nine months of carrying the child."

What do you think of the strings that are tied to a relationship with the Holy Ghost? Does this impose a stiff responsibility on you that you do not want to bear? What kind of a commitment do you need to make with the Holy Ghost to revitalize an intimate relationship with Him?

DAY 27

WHO ARE YOU INWARDLY?

The spirit of man is the candle of the Lord, searching all the inward parts of the belly (Proverbs 20:27).

Excerpt: *Release Your Anointing Expanded Edition*, Chapter 6.

Man is made in God's image and likeness. We are also a triune being—body, soul, and spirit. God has saved our spirits. Our bodies are not saved. The body does not want to be holy or bring forth good fruit. Your body will never tell you to pray. The body will never encourage you to live right. The body will never restrain you from gossiping. The body is flesh and will always be flesh.

David prayed, *"Search me, O God, and know my heart: try me, and know my thoughts"* (Ps. 139:23).

What does God use to search us? Read Proverbs 20:27 again. This verse shows us three truths:

1.   Man is not only body and soul, but also spirit.

2.   The spirit of man is the candle of the Lord.

3. The Lord uses this spirit to search the innermost being of humans.

Underneath your shout, your dance, your speaking in tongues, who are you really? This has always been the problem with man-made holiness. Trying to change a person outwardly only leaves him or her frustrated, confused, and feeling like a failure.

God does just the opposite. He changes you from the inside out.

Your Thoughts

1. If you were to explain how you were created in God's image, what would you say? How are you made in His likeness?

_____

_____

_____

_____

_____

_____

2. What is the difference between the body and the soul? What do you think makes up the soul of a person? What is the difference between the soul and the spirit? How do all three of these make up who you are?

_____

_____

_____

3. What limitations does your body impose or try to impose on your soul? How does your body get in the way of your spirit? What must you do to overcome your body's limitations?

_____

_____

4. Is it unsettling to you to be like David and invite God to search you thoroughly? Why or why not? Why is it important for us to invite God to search us?

_____

_____

_____

5. What does Proverbs 20:27 speak to your heart about your spirit? How does your innermost part truly reflect who you are as opposed to the outward appearance you have?

_____

_____

_____

_____

Meditation

"Changing from the outside in has no lasting effect. It always leaves the womb barren, crying, 'It's not enough!' Changing from the outside in is like painting a building without removing the trash that clutters the inside.

"There is a difference between repainting and _repenting_. _Repainting_ changes the outside, repenting changes the inside."

Have you ever repainted a situation instead of repenting? The trouble with repainting is eventually the paint peels away leaving the original problem. Do you remember a problem that you thought was taken care of only to have it reemerge? Could repenting rather than repainting have solved the problem the first time?

DAY 28

OUR SPIRITS ARE JOINED

The Spirit itself beareth witness with our spirit, that we are the children of God (Romans 8:16).

Excerpt: *Release Your Anointing Expanded Edition*, Chapter 6.

This Scripture deals with two spirits—the spirit of man and the Holy Spirit. Joined together at salvation, the Holy Spirit testifies to our spirit that we are saved. He can testify in your spirit when all hell is breaking loose.

Have you ever wanted something and knew it was God's will, but you just couldn't seem to get a breakthrough? As you see someone with the very thing you want, it causes a kicking inside you. This lets you know that your baby is still there. You haven't aborted or miscarried. The Holy Spirit lets you know it's still in you.

What happens next is simply awesome. The Holy Spirit becomes so much of a part of your life that you begin to have more than just a Sunday morning fling with Him. You begin to know the Holy Spirit and understand His purpose. You become sensitive to His feelings, which keep you from grieving the Holy Spirit. You begin to feel a burning love and appreciation for the

Holy Spirit, which helps you to obey and submit to His leading. This keeps the flame of spiritual passion burning in your spirit.

Your Thoughts

1. What is the difference between the spirit of a man and the Spirit of God? How do they work together within us?

_____

_____

_____

_____

2. How has the Holy Ghost worked inside you to testify to your salvation? How has He given you a witness during trials or challenges?

_____

_____

_____

_____

3. When we have a desire, how do we know that it is God's will for us? When we know the desire is God's will, how does the Holy Spirit give us a witness? How does this bring confidence to our souls?

_____

_____

_____

_____

4. Have you ever been so infatuated with someone that it was hard to concentrate because of the mini day-dreams you had about your relationship? In what way do you think we should be so in love with God, that the Holy Spirit overwhelms us in even a greater way?

_____

_____

_____

_____

5. As in a relationship with a close friend or spouse, we begin to "read their minds," how does regular, frequent intimacy with the Holy Ghost allow us to know the mind of God?

_____

_____

_____

_____

_____

Meditation

"As a result of your daily communion with the Holy Spirit, the barren areas in your life that have cried out for years—the spiritual womb that has never been satisfied—now becomes impregnated by the Holy Spirit.... We supply the womb; the Holy Ghost supplies the seed; our relationship with God brings about conception. As we bring forth spiritual offspring, they should resemble the Father."

Think through the process of an intimate relationship with the Holy Ghost. How has this process occurred in your life? What stage is your relationship in at present?

DAY 29

THERMOMETER OR THERMOSTAT?

But the fruit of the Spirit is love, joy, peace, longsuffering, gentleness, goodness, faith, meekness, temperance: against such there is no law (Galatians 5:22-23).

Excerpt: *Release Your Anointing Expanded Edition*, Chapter 6.

The Holy Ghost functions like a thermostat and a thermometer. The thermometer reflects its surrounding temperature, and the thermostat controls the inside heating system that gives the thermometer its reading.

In the same way, the Holy Ghost works inside you. Your outward actions reflect your temperature to those around you.

Galatians 5:22-23 describes three sets of triplets:

1. Atmosphere.

2. Attitude.

3. Attribute.

The atmosphere is your surroundings. The Holy Spirit will build a fire of His own that will bring warmth to a cold atmosphere. This is why the first three triplets—love, joy, and peace—are atmosphere-changing fruit.

The second three triplets—longsuffering, gentleness, goodness—are attitude-changing fruit. God sometimes lets us go through difficult situations to let us see what's really inside us.

An attribute is simply a personality or character trait. We call this third triplet—faith, meekness, and self-control—attribute fruit because these qualities cannot be attributed to you but only to the Holy Ghost.

Within you lies the ability to become whatever you choose to be. Remember that you have a choice, and the choice does not come without a price.

Your Thoughts

1. What's your spiritual temperature? Are you hot or cold or lukewarm? What would others say your spiritual temperature currently is?

_____

_____

_____

2. Think through the atmospheres around you at home, at work, in your ministry area, or in any of your regular endeavors. How has the Holy Spirit used love, joy, and/or peace to change the atmosphere around you in those activities?

_____

_____

_____

_____

3. How would other people assess your attitude during times of great blessing? What would they say about your attitude during times of trial? Why are longsuffering, gentleness, and goodness important to your life right now?

_____

_____

_____

_____

_____

4. Are you someone whom God would describe as bearing His character? How would you score on a report card in the subjects of faith, meekness, or self-control?

_____

_____

_____

_____

5. "Within you lies the ability to become whatever you choose to be." What does this statement mean to you personally? Why do our choices have price tags attached? What might some of these price tags be?

_____

_____

_____

_____

Meditation

"You have a strength that defies human logic. You have an ability to stand that you cannot attribute to anyone but God. You have a peace that even the apostle Paul couldn't understand, so he called it the *"peace of God, which passeth all understanding"* (Phil. 4:7). You have a joy that the apostle Peter could not describe, so he called it *"joy unspeakable and full of glory"* (I Pet. 1:8)."

Have you experienced the peace that passes all understanding? Think about one of those times and thank God for His mercy and grace. Have you experienced unspeakable, glorious joy? Think about one of those times and thank God for His love and faithfulness.

DAY 30

FRUIT AND PATIENCE

Verily, verily, I say unto you, except a corn of wheat fall into the ground and die, it abideth alone: but if it die, it bringeth forth much fruit (John 12:24).

Excerpt: *Release Your Anointing Expanded Edition*, Chapter 6.

Truth can be seen in the physical and spiritual realms. Jesus illustrated a dynamic spiritual truth with the seed example. The outer casing of a seed has only one purpose: to house the heart of the grain, which produces new life.

This outer casing is like our flesh, which houses our soul and spirit. As we *"crucify the flesh"* (Gal. 5:24) and *"seek those things which are above"* (Col. 3:1), the life of the Spirit comes to full fruition in us.

We can confidently say:

I am crucified with Christ: nevertheless I live; yet not I, but Christ liveth in me: and the life which I now live in the flesh I live by the faith of the Son of God, who loved me, and gave Himself for me (Galatians 2:20).

Your Thoughts

I. Have you died to your flesh? Are you taking steps in that direction? Is this a yearly, monthly, daily, or moment-by-moment death?

_____

_____

_____

_____

_____

2. Will being "crucified with Christ" bring death to your flesh? How will your faith flourish if you can put to death your fleshly desires?

_____

_____

_____

_____

_____

3. Have you known people who seem to have no problem defeating satan's temptations? Do you think they constantly rely on the Holy Ghost? Or are they falling apart from within?

_____

_____

_____

_____

_____

4. Are you patient enough to wait for the new life to sprout from you?

_____

_____

_____

_____

_____

5. What exciting new growth have you experienced since dying to sin? Are you taking an active role in nurturing that new growth?

_____

_____

_____

_____

Meditation

"Stop your Adamic nature from being the dominate force in your life.... In Numbers 17:1-8 God took something seemingly dead (Aaron's rod) and caused it to bud. You may long to function and produce.... Within every one of us is a spirit that cries out as Jacob, 'I know I am Jacob now, but within me is the desire to become Israel!'"

Producing fruit takes patience and the Holy Spirit. How delicious are fresh fruits—plump red strawberries in the spring, juicy watermelons in the summer, golden apples in the fall. Each takes time to become ripe and ready for picking. In the meantime are you feeding and nurturing your spirit, mind, and soul with the Word of God?

DAY 31

COME UP HIGHER

After this I looked, and, behold, a door was opened in heaven: and the first voice which I heard was as it were of a trumpet talking to me; which said, Come up hither, and I will shew thee things which must be hereafter (Revelation 4:1).

Excerpt: *Release Your Anointing Expanded Edition*, Chapter 7.

He that hath an ear, let him hear what the Spirit saith unto the churches (Revelation 3:6).

What the Spirit reveals is totally awesome. The scope of God's blessing covers what eye has not seen and what ear has not heard. It gets even more mind-blowing than that! The storehouse of God's will for our lives includes blessings that we have never even thought about—things that surpass even our wildest imaginations; things that have never even entered our hearts. That's awesome!

But God hath revealed them unto us by His Spirit: for the Spirit searcheth all things, yea, the deep things of God (1 Corinthians 2:10).

The apostle Paul calls them "the deep things of God." Many of us never get past the first oracles or the starting place with God.

The storehouse of Heaven is full. You will never exhaust its inventory of glory. If we aren't walking in such a way to access it, however, these glorious realities will never occur in our lives.

Therefore, leaving the principles of the doctrine of Christ, let us go on unto perfection (Hebrews 6:1a).

We must move away from where we first started with God.

Your Thoughts

1. Since we all have ears, what ear is Revelation 3:6 referring to? How do we hear with this ear?

_____

_____

_____

_____

2. What has the Spirit revealed to you that is totally awe-some? How can we access God's storehouse in a way that we are blessed beyond our wildest imaginations?

_____

_____

3. What do you think the "deep things of God" are? What do you think it means that the "Spirit search-est all things"?

_____

_____

_____

4. Do you feel like you have moved beyond where you started with God? In what ways have you moved for-ward? Have there been times when you have not moved forward the way God wanted?

_____

_____

_____

5. How do we access the storehouse of Heaven? What glory do we receive as we move beyond the basics in the Kingdom?

_____

_____

_____

_____

_____

_____

Meditation

"Many Christians never access the windows of Heaven because they are still living in the outer court and have never broken through to the third dimension, the holy of holies. Many live in defeat and carnality because they have remained on the same level where they first boarded the ark of salvation."

How well do you access the windows of Heaven? Do you feel like you regularly go to the holy of holies? Take some time to consider what God wants you to do to come up higher.

DAY 32

MESSAGES TO SEVEN CHURCHES— Part I: Jesus in the Midst

"The mystery of the seven stars that you saw in my right hand and of the seven golden lampstands is this: The seven stars are the angels of the seven churches, and the seven lampstands are the seven churches" (Revelation 1:20 NIV).

Excerpt: *Release Your Anointing Expanded Edition*, Chapter 7.

In Revelation 2:1, Jesus walked in the midst of the church at Ephesus. In Revelation 3:20, He stands on the outside knocking for an entrance. This shows the digression of the church. Each one of these churches depicts our life as a child of God at one time or another.

1. We have left our first love (see Rev. 2:4).

2. We have been crushed as the church of Smyrna, a city noted for its perfume or myrrh (see Rev. 2:8).

3. We have had the spirit of Pergamos in us, which has caused others to stumble (see Rev. 2:14).

4. We have things in us that were strong but now have begun to die, as is the case with the church of Sardis (see Rev. 3:2).

This revelation came as a result of the seven spirits of God and seven stars. The seven spirits denote perfection or completion. It is not seven different spirits, but shows the fullness of one Spirit (see Isa. 11:2). The seven stars denote the ministers. The word they preached, in conjunction with the Spirit, brought about this revelation to the churches (see Rev. 1:20).

Your Thoughts

I. Why does Revelation 3:20 show the digression of the church? Why do you think the church has left Jesus out of its ministry?

_____

_____

_____

_____

_____

2. What is "first love"? What characterizes this type of love? Is this true of you?

_____

_____

_____

3. Have you ever felt crushed like the church in Smyrna? What are some ways in which the world can crush you? What about the church or other Christians?

_____

_____

_____

4. Would the Lord ever tell you that you had caused someone to stumble? What does this mean? What do you think is at the core of influencing someone else away from the gospel?

_____

_____

_____

5. Is the accusation against the church of Sardis part of
   your life or someone you know? What creates a
   short-term Christian? Why do you think endurance
   is so difficult?

_____

_____

_____

_____

Meditation

"Revelation from God comes in three segments: past, present,
and future. First, God sometimes reveals things in our past for
instruction or edification. Jesus told the apostle John on the isle of
Patmos, '*Write the things which thou hast seen* [past], *and the things which are*
[present]...*Sometimes God reaches into your storm or dilemma and tells you
everything will be all right. Write...the things which shall be hereafter* [future]'
(Rev. 1:19)."

Has God ever explained your past to you? Has He allowed you
to see His perspective of the present part of your life? Has He
ever explained your future? Consider what you must do to be in
the place to receive revelations from the Lord.

DAY 33

MESSAGES TO SEVEN CHURCHES— Part 2: He Knows Us

"To the angel of the church in Saris write: These are the words of him who holds the seven spirits of God and the seven stars. I know your deeds; you have a reputation of being alive, but you are dead" (Revelation 3:1NIV).

Excerpt: *Release Your Anointing Expanded Edition*, Chapter 7.

Let's look at the message given to the churches in Revelation, chapters 2 and 3:

1. God says to the churches, "I know." These are humbling—even frightening—words. Just think of all there is to know about you. God says, "I know."

2. God says, "I know thy works." God looks beyond surface appearance and says, "I know what others do not know because I know the heart."

3. God says, "I know your name." God knows our name or reputation. Did you know that God knows your name and still loves you? He can know your reputation and still use you. He can know who you really are behind that worship, behind that song, behind that dance, behind your tongues, behind your preaching.

4. God sees beyond the name to the reality. Death means a separation, to cut off. It's like turning a light switch to the off position, which breaks the circuit and cuts off the power. God says, "I know that you are separated from life. Your name may say differently, but I know."

5. God also reveals a blessing. Something remained to work with.

Your Thoughts

1. Is it disconcerting to realize that God knows you inside and out, that every hidden place is open to Him? How can these words be frightening? How could these words be humbling?

_____

_____

_____

2. Isn't it incredible that God knows every work you have done, whether in secret or openly expressed? Since we don't need to remind Him of every good thing we have done, does it make it exciting for Him to look into your heart and your true intentions? Or does this make you feel uneasy?

_____

_____

_____

_____

3. How important is it to you to have a "good name," a reputation that shines? Are there some people who may praise you and others who may not think so highly of you? Is it comforting to know that God sees beyond what others think?

_____

_____

_____

_____

4. When people think highly of you, can you tell the difference between praise and flattery? When people criticize you, do you see the difference between the truth someone may share and the condemnation that is not of God? Why do we have to die to what others think and say?

_____

_____

_____

_____

5. After God has seen your insides, looked through your good works, peered beyond your reputation, and allowed you to die to yourself, how does He find something remaining with which He can work? What are areas of purity that He can work with inside of you?

_____

_____

_____

_____

Meditation

"God says, 'I know the truth. I know your name.' God knows that your name is Jacob but still asks, 'What is thy name?' Anytime an all-wise, all-knowing God asks a question, it isn't for His benefit. You need to confess, 'My name is Jacob.'"

Even though He knows your name, He wants you to confess it because He is going to change your name and speak a glorious destiny over you.

Think about how Jacob was before and after he wrestled with the angel. God knew his deceit and still wanted to use him. Why does Jacob's answer of telling his name help us understand how the transformation can take place for each of us?

DAY 34

MESSAGES TO SEVEN CHURCHES— Part 3: Be Watchful

Be watchful, and strengthen the things which remain, that are ready to die: for I have not found thy works perfect before God (Revelation 3:2).

Excerpt: *Release Your Anointing Expanded Edition*, Chapter 7.

- "Be watchful." The word *watchful* means to awaken or arouse something that is at the point of dying. It isn't dead yet. If the Holy Spirit said these things that remained were ready to die, there was still a little life left.

Maybe you have felt that your ministry is dead. If you feel any kick at all, you need to be aroused and to awaken, because the movement tells you it's still alive.

- "Strengthen the things that remain." The word *strengthen* means to solidify, to establish, to set upright again; to take something that has been weakened and build it back up.

Apostle Paul said, *"Most gladly therefore will I rather glory in my infirmities, that the power of Christ may rest upon me"* (2 Cor. 12:9).

When his strength had given out and his resources were exhausted, he had no other place to turn. He could rely on no other strength but the strength that God gave him.

Your own strength is not enough, but if you will take what's left of it and give it to God, Who is more than enough, you will find Him to be sufficient.

Your Thoughts

I. Is there something in your life that is at the point of dying? When something is ready to die within us, why does the Lord ask us to be watchful?

_____

_____

_____

_____

_____

2. Have you ever felt as if you were just going through the motions in ministry or that God's grace had lifted from a once-thriving ministry? What must we do to arouse the life that still remains?

_____

_____

_____

_____

3. The phrases used to describe the word *strengthen* show what we can do when things seem to be waning. What does it take to solidify a ministry endeavor? What might be necessary in order to set a relationship or ministry upright again? What are some steps that could be used so you can build up the weakened area?

_____

_____

_____

_____

4. What does Paul mean in Second Corinthians 12:9?
    Is he a masochist? What key in this verse can turn
    around our attitude? Our perception of the chal-
    lenge? Our hope for the future? Our rationale as to
    what good the problem can create?

    _____

    _____

    _____

    _____

    _____

5. Compare and contrast your own strength with the
    strength of God. What part of solving issues is
    assigned to God? What part is assigned to you?

    _____

    _____

    _____

    _____

    _____

Meditation

"Within you are gifts, callings, and talents that have been weakened, pressed down, or held back. Your vision, dream, or desire may have been crushed. You may not have had any control over the circumstances. Perhaps your disobedience grieved the Holy Spirit. But arise, my friend! Whatever the devil did to you, he didn't complete the job. He left some strength in you."

What gifts, callings, or talents do you have that have been weakened, pressed down, or held back? Do you have visions, dreams, or desires that have been crushed? Spend time asking the Lord to forgive any disobedience in your life. Ask the Holy Spirit to build up the strength that remains within you.

DAY 35

ARISE! TIME TO TAKE INVENTORY

---

*And Jesus answering said, A certain man went down from Jerusalem to Jericho, and fell among thieves, which stripped him of his raiment, and wounded him, and departed, leaving him **half dead** (Luke 10:30).*

Excerpt: *Release Your Anointing Expanded Edition*, Chapter 7.

In the parable of the Good Samaritan, Jesus said the thieves left the man "half dead." His enemies made a big mistake. They left the man with just enough life to revive. He came back to life.

God knows you are a 911 case. God knows you are in critical condition. In spite of your dilemma, He says, "It's not over until I say it's over." You may have been diagnosed with a terminal illness. Place your case in the hands of the Great Physician. Refuse to accept the verdict. Get a second opinion.

When you have healthy thoughts about your own identity, it frees you from the need to impress other people. Their opinion ceases to be the shrine where you worship! While we dress and smell nice outwardly, people do not hear the constant hammering and sawing going on inwardly as the Lord works within us, trying desperately to meet a deadline and present us as a newly constructed masterpiece fit for the Master's use.

Your Thoughts

1. Satan would love to see you say last rites over your dreams or your ministry. What can you do to stop him from achieving his goal?

_____

_____

_____

2. How can you take hold of the leftovers of your life and turn them into a meal fit to serve the King?

_____

_____

_____

3. The man helped by the Good Samaritan was "half dead." Do you feel as if you are half dead some days? The Holy Spirit within you is ready to breathe a big breath of fresh, pure air into your lungs—are you ready to receive it?

    _____

    _____

    _____

4. When you take inventory of your life, do you list all of the blessings you have, or do you focus on the negative aspects of your life?

    _____

    _____

5. What does "God knows" mean to you?

    _____

    _____

    _____

    _____

Meditation

"You don't have to pretend. God knows everything isn't all right. God knows you aren't on top of the situation. God knows. ...In the midst of your trial, dilemma, or storm, do you still find a desire to overcome? Do you refuse to take no for an answer? He can take everything you have lost—your time, joy, and integrity—and bring you right up to date as though it never happened."

Arise! Take inventory of your life from God's perspective. He sees you as treasure beyond compare. How does His perspective line up with yours?

DAY 36

GOD'S LAYAWAY PLAN

In whom ye also trusted, after that ye heard the word of truth, the gospel of your salvation: in whom also after that ye believed, ye were sealed with that holy Spirit of promise, which is the earnest of our inheritance until the redemption of the purchased possession, unto the praise of His glory (Ephesians 1:13-14).

Excerpt: *Release Your Anointing Expanded Edition*, Chapter 8.

How can you keep going when all hell has been unleashed against you? If our generation will usher in the coming of the Lord—and I believe prophecy indicates we will—then we must be equipped to face the onslaught of the devil.

Paul penned the words of Ephesians, the first of his prison letters, from the confines of a Roman jail. Despite his circumstances, Paul viewed life from an eternal perspective.

The Greek word for earnest in Ephesians 1:13-14 is *arrhabon*, meaning a "pledge, a down payment, a security deposit." It's an amount paid in advance to secure the transaction until the full price is paid to complete the purchase.

If you've ever bought merchandise on layaway, you place a down payment on your goods with the promise to pay the full amount. In your case, God wants you enough that He paid earnest money to secure the transaction. When the devil offers you the world, God says, "Sorry, devil. I began the transaction, and I will finish it! I sealed it with a promise. The transaction will not be complete until I redeem the body. Until that day comes, I own all rights. This is mine."

Your Thoughts

I. Have you ever felt that all hell had been unleashed against you? What kind of preparation do we need to face onslaughts of the enemy in the future?

_____

_____

2. Think through Ephesians I:13-14 and put each phrase into your own "amplified" version, personalizing what it means to you.

_____

_____

_____

3. What kind of deposit has God made on your life?
   What security has He put down to seal the initial
   transaction?

   _____

   _____

   _____

   _____

4. What comfort do you have in the fact that God fin-
   ishes what He begins? How does this assurance allow
   you to focus on "running the race" rather than worrying about whether you are in the race or not?

   _____

   _____

   _____

   _____

   _____

5. When will God redeem us? Until then, does the devil have any rights to you? Do you have any rights to yourself? Why do you belong to God?

_____

_____

_____

_____

_____

Meditation

"If we see a piece of property that we want but do not have the entire price, we can put a deposit or a down payment on it. Both parties understand that a portion of the payment is still owed. This merely declares to other interested parties that the property already has a purchaser. To confirm the desire to purchase, the potential owner has given earnest money or a security deposit."

Spiritually speaking, what kind of mortgage does God have on you? Do you see yourself as a spiritual investment of God's portfolio? Pray that the Lord will open your heart to understand how much value you have to Him.

DAY 37

NOT WITHOUT A PRICE

For a just man falleth seven times, and riseth up again: but the wicked shall fall into mischief (Proverbs 24:16).

Excerpt: *Release Your Anointing Expanded Edition*, Chapter 8.

If you ever get around people who have accomplished much, they will tell you that those accomplishments didn't come without a price. Generally, that cost is much more expensive than you normally want to pay.

The real price of success lies within the need to persevere. The trophy is never given to someone who does not complete the task. Setbacks are just set-ups for God to show what He is able to do. Funerals are for people who have accepted the thought that everything is over. Don't do that; instead, tell the enemy, "I am not dead yet."

Jesus seldom attended funerals. When He did, it was to arrest death and stop the ceremony. The Lord doesn't like pity parties, and those who have them are shocked to find that although He is invited, He seldom attends.

The whole theme of Christianity is one of rising again. However, you can't rise until you fall. That doesn't mean you should fall into sin. It means you should allow the resurrecting power of the Holy Ghost to operate in your life, regardless of whether you have fallen into sin, discouragement, apathy, or fear.

Your Thoughts

1. Have you ever thrown yourself a pity party? Did you expect Jesus to show up? Did He?

_____

_____

_____

2. What is the cost of transforming yourself into the person God wants you to be? Are you willing to pay that cost? Why?

_____

_____

_____

_____

3. There is a certain safety in being dormant. Do you ever feel as if being dormant is better than reaching out and taking a risk? Can goals be achieved by inactivity?

_____

_____

_____

_____

4. Have you paid a high price for something you wanted and then after you got it home you quickly tired of it? Paying the cost of being God's child comes with eternal rewards—name some.

_____

_____

_____

_____

_____

5. How hard is it to rise after a fall? Do you keep track
    of how many times you have had to pick yourself
    up? God will always soften your landing if you ask
    Him; He will always give you His hand to lift you
    up. Do you believe this truth?

_____

_____

_____

_____

Meditation

"There are obstacles that can trip you as you escalate toward productivity. But it doesn't matter what tripped you; it matters that you rise up.... Regardless of what causes us to fall, what matters it that we get up!... The Holy Spirit challenges us to stand in the midst of contrary winds, and if we stumble to our knees, to grasp the hand of God's grace and arise."

All of us will fall—it is up to us to decide whether we will rise up again. Faith will keep us dependent on His strength. Love will keep us focused on Him. Hope will give us the power to release our anointing.

DAY 38

RELENTLESS

And not only they, but ourselves also, which have the firstfruits of the Spirit, even we ourselves groan within ourselves, waiting for the adoption, to wit, the redemption of our body (Romans 8:23).

Excerpt: *Release Your Anointing Expanded Edition*, Chapter 8.

Relentless is the word I use to describe people who will not take no for an answer. They try things one way, and if that doesn't work, they try it another way. You who are about to break beneath the stress of intense struggles, be relentless. Do not quit!

A terrible thing happens to people who give up too easily. It is called *regret*. It is the nagging, gnawing feeling that says, "If I had tried harder, I could have succeeded."

Granted, we all experience some degree of failure. That is how we learn and grow. The problem is when we fail to question if it was our lack of commitment that allowed us to forfeit an opportunity to turn the test into a triumph! We can never be sure of the answer unless we rally our talents, muster our courage, have faith and hope, and focus our strength to achieve a goal.

Many of you are near a breakthrough in your life. You may have fought for years to get to where you are with God. Many of you are pregnant with destiny. You are carrying within the womb of your spirit a ministry that could change the world.

Your Thoughts

1. Define the word *relentless* in your own words. Have you ever been relentless about a personal goal or pursuit? What gave you the drive to press ahead, no matter what?

_____

_____

_____

2. When challenges occur, how do relentless people react? How does the process of trial and error produce innovations and stronger people? Do you react to challenges with a relentless spirit?

_____

_____

_____

3. Have you any regrets about your life thus far? What has created those regrets? How can you prevent future regrets?

_____

_____

_____

_____

_____

4. What are some things that you have tried and failed? How did you feel about those failures? Were they easy to accept? Have you ever been able to turn a failure into a triumph? What made the difference?

_____

_____

_____

_____

_____

5. Since we do not know the future, we could be on the edge of a breakthrough and not know it. How does this possibility motivate us to move forward in a storm?

_____

_____

_____

_____

Meditation

"We must understand the working of the Holy Spirit. Many become discouraged when they fall short of their goals as a child of God."

The spirit is saved by faith, and the body is saved by hope. Hope purifies our soul. When it doesn't look good, hope says, "It's all right." This is why we need a strong witness in our soul. God gives us hope in the midst of our storm.

How is your spirit saved by faith? How is your body saved by hope? Pray that the Lord increases your faith and your hope. Receive the comfort and peace that only the Lord can provide.

DAY 39

GOD INHABITS
AN OLD HOUSE

But I keep under my body, and bring it into subjection: lest that by any means, when I have preached to others, I myself should be a castaway (1 Corinthians 9:27).

Excerpt: *Release Your Anointing Expanded Edition*, Chapter 8.

Within our decaying shells, we constantly peel away, by faith, the lusts and jealousies that adorn the walls of our hearts. If the angels were to stroll through the earth with the Creator and ask, "Which house is Yours?" He would pass by all the mansions and cathedrals. Unashamedly, He would point at you and me and say, "That is Mine!" We who blunder and stumble in our humanity continually wrestle with the knowledge that *our God has put so much in so little!*

Despite all our washing and painting, all our grooming and exercising, this old house is still falling apart. There is no doubt that we have been saved, and there is no doubt that *the house is haunted.* The Holy Ghost Himself resides beneath this sagging roof.

This divine occupation is not an act of a desperate guest who, having no place else to stay, chose this impoverished site as a temporary place to "ride out" the storm. No, God Himself has—of His own free will and predetermined purpose—put us in the embarrassing situation of entertaining a Guest whose lofty stature so far exceeds us that we hardly know how to serve Him!

Your Thoughts

1. Why do you think God has chosen our rickety shells in which to house His Spirit? What does this show about God's love for humanity?

_____

_____

_____

2. How does One who is so perfect live in squalor within our dying frame? Does this knowledge humble you? Do you receive encouragement by knowing that within you resides Someone who can outperform anyone on earth?

_____

_____

_____

3. Are there surface areas in your life that you have attempted to whitewash and secure, while something was rotting underneath? Think through this question carefully. Let God reveal what you may have tried to cover without addressing the root cause.

_____

_____

_____

_____

_____

4. How should we "take care" of our Guest? What should we do to serve Him?

_____

_____

_____

_____

_____

5. How would you explain the indwelling of the Holy Spirit to a new Christian? What impact has the Spirit made on your life so you can give testimony firsthand as to His occupation in your temple?

_____

_____

_____

_____

_____

Meditation

"I pay very little attention to those among us who feel obligated to impress us with the ludicrous idea that they have already attained what is meant to be a lifelong pursuit. The renewal of the old person is a daily exercise of the heart. It progressively strengthens the character day by day, not overnight!"

Have you ever met someone who thought they had already attained their lifelong pursuit? Do these kinds of people continue to grow past the place where they think they have "arrived?" What do we need to do to keep a teachable spirit so we continually grow toward God's future for us?

DAY 40

STRIPPED DOWN
TO THE ETERNAL

So He got up from the meal, took off His outer clothing, and wrapped a towel around His waist (John 13:4 NIV).

Excerpt: *Release Your Anointing Expanded Edition*, Chapter 8.

Jesus laid aside His garments. That is what ministry is all about. It requires you to lay aside your garments. Lay aside your personal ambitions. Ministry is birthed when you are stripped down to your heart's desire, when beneath every other thread of whimsical grandeur, your heart says, I want my life to have counted for something. *I want to accomplish something for God.*

Have you ever prayed, "Oh God, don't let me impress anyone else but the One to whom I gave my life"?

Have we given our lives to the Lord? Then why are we still standing around the table arguing over who is going to sit on the left and who is going to sit on the right? *Why have we not laid aside our garments?*

You can never be really anointed until you personally experience a situation that calls you to lay aside your garments. It is from this that the tears of worship are born. They fall lavishly down a face that has been pulled from behind its covering and laid bare before God. Who can help but worship Him, once we see Him aside from every distraction and weight?

Your Thoughts

I. If you had been with the disciples when Jesus began to wash their feet, how do you think you would have reacted? Would you have been embarrassed or confused? Would our reactions have been different from the disciples?

_____

_____

_____

_____

_____

_____

2. How much do you want your life to count for in the Kingdom? How greatly do you desire to do something for God? Are you willing to set aside what you think this means, and listen to what God thinks?

_____

_____

_____

_____

_____

3. When we give our lives over to the Lord, what kind of ownership decision have we made in terms of our bodies, souls, and spirits? What rights does the Owner have over us? Do we have any rights?

_____

_____

_____

_____

_____

4. Why is *anointed* so connected with *humility* in service? Why are these paramount to a deeper anointing?

_____

_____

_____

_____

_____

_____

5. How does worship affect your life? Do you ever find yourself naked and laid bare before the Lord during worship? Is this important so we can see God clearly and commune with Him face to face?

_____

_____

_____

_____

_____

Meditation

"The garment represents different things to different people. It is whatever camouflages our realness, whatever hinders us from really affecting our environment. Our garments are the personal agendas that we have set for ourselves. Like the fig leaves sewn together in the garden, we have contrived our own coverings. The terrible tragedy of it all is that sooner or later, whatever we have sown together will ultimately be stripped away."

What garments are you currently wearing that need to be laid aside so you can serve God? What agendas do you need to put on hold? How will God honor your service to Him?

THOUGHTS & REFLECTIONS

_____

_____

_____

_____

_____

_____

_____

_____

_____

_____

_____

_____

_____

_____

_____

_____

_____

_____

_____

_____

_____

_____

_____

_____

_____

_____

_____

_____

_____

_____

_____

_____

_____

_____

_____

_____

_____

_____

_____

_____

_____

_____

_____

_____

_____

_____

_____

_____

_____

_____

_____

_____

_____

_____

_____

_____

_____

_____

_____

_____

_____

_____

_____

_____

_____

_____

_____

_____

_____

_____

_____

_____

_____

_____

_____

_____

_____

_____

_____

_____

_____

_____

_____

_____

_____

Additional copies of this book and other
book titles from DESTINY IMAGE are
available at your local bookstore.

Call toll-free: 1-800-722-6774.

Send a request for a catalog to:

Destiny Image® Publishers, Inc.

P.O. Box 310
Shippensburg, PA 17257-0310

"Speaking to the Purposes of God for This
Generation and for the Generations to Come."

For a complete list of our titles,
visit us at www.destinyimage.com.